Lessons Learned at

216

Lessons Learned at

Carol Bruce-Lockhart

iUniverse

LESSONS LEARNED AT 216

Scripture quotations marked NIV are taken from the Holy Bible, New International Version®. NIV®. Copyright © 1973, 1978, 1984 by International Bible Society. Used by permission of Zondervan. All rights reserved. [Biblica]

Scripture quotations marked TLB are taken from The Living Bible copyright © 1971. Used by permission of Tyndale House Publishers, Inc., Carol Stream, Illinois 60188. All rights reserved.

Scripture quotations marked KJV are from the Holy Bible, King James Version (Authorized Version). First published in 1611. Quoted from the KJV Classic Reference Bible, Copyright © 1983 by The Zondervan Corporation.

Scripture quotations marked NASB are taken from the New American Standard Bible®, Copyright © 1960, 1962, 1963, 1968, 1971, 1972, 1973, 1975, 1977, 1995 by The Lockman Foundation. Used by permission.

iUniverse books may be ordered through booksellers or by contacting:

iUniverse
1663 Liberty Drive
Bloomington, IN 47403
www.iuniverse.com
844-349-9409

ISBN: 978-1-6632-1083-8 (sc)
ISBN: 978-1-6632-1082-1 (e)

Library of Congress Control Number: 2020924605

Print information available on the last page.

iUniverse rev. date: 12/18/2020

A word of thanks...

To my siblings Belinda, Wayne, Pam, Cheryl, Yvonne, Tiffany and Talisha (who are at the center of many of my stories) for trusting me to present our childhood adventures in a respectful way. Also, to my parents Otis and Louise Bruce Jr., for raising us in an atmosphere that created the opportunity for many memories. To my grandmother, Mina Reece who never failed to represent herself as the strong spiritual foundation in our lives. To my children Miriam, Malisse, Aaron, and other beloved family members who were my sounding boards over the years as I repeatedly recited our family tales. And to my husband Theodus who has been by my side for 42 years and, who lovingly suffered through burnt fish sticks, Peanut Butter and Jelly sandwiches, and fast foods over the past few months as I toiled to bring this book into fruition.

Last, but certainly not least, I am grateful to God for His leadership, love, and protection. You have always been with me from the very beginning, even before I knew you. Thank you for the gift of words that have been entrusted to me. I pray that I use my words wisely as a means of uplifting all who read them.

I love you all!
Carol

Carol (Age 4)

Contents

Introduction

Cheryl's Day

The back door slowly opened, its rusted hinges squealing with each push. Momma leaned out and yelled, "Watch your sister Cheryl!" Then she said to Cheryl, "You are to play up here and not back by the fire!" Cheryl bounded down the steps, her crisp plaid dress rustling in the wind while her long thick ponytails bounced on her back with every step. She went straight to the swing set in the middle of the yard.

It was trash day, and back then, our Dad had opted to burn our trash instead of having the city pick it up. We all had daily duties that we were responsible for in our home. Belinda and I had to sweep and mop the floors and washed and dry dishes. My brother, Wayne's duties were to feed our dog Ringo and empty and burn the trash. Our two young sisters' only charge was to play and have fun all day, and many times we were forced to be their toys.

Cheryl skipped over to the swing set and whined for one of us to push her. My sister Belinda and I took turns pushing her as she laughed and squealed, "Higher, Higher!" Wayne was at the far end of the back-yard dancing back and forth around the fire while using a long wooden pole to poke at the contents of the burning can, making sure that nothing fell out.

The barrel had gotten extremely hot and was now quickly eating the trash within its belly. We had walked away from Cheryl for just a moment to watch Wayne at the back of the yard. But when we turned to check on her, we saw that she was no longer on the swings, but had followed us and was now standing just steps from the flaming barrel entirely captivated by the flames.

Wayne yelled at her to get away, but it was too late. As Cheryl turned to run, an ember of fire shot out of the barrel and landed on the back of her pretty plaid dress. Immediately her clothing went up in flames! Cheryl let out a loud shrill and took off running towards the house crying loudly for Momma. Wayne immediately sprinted after her, caught her, threw her to the ground, and rolled her back and forth to extinguish the angry flames. We had recently learned fire safety in school and had been taught to "Stop, Drop and Roll" if we were on fire. So, lucky for Cheryl, Wayne knew just what to do.

Momma must have heard Cheryl's scream and was now hurrying from the house. She quickly grabbed Cheryl and cradled her into her arms. We all noticed that the back of Cheryl's dress was completely gone! Momma frantically began dusting the dirt off Cheryl's back. Miraculously not a burn was found; not even on her beautiful long ponytails! Momma hugged her tightly, gratefully relieved that she was safe.

Fortunately, my sister escaped her ordeal without experiencing any physical harm. It is hard to fathom how she survived the flames without experiencing a single injury. But even as children, we understood that it had to have been God's special protection. We all learned a "Life Lesson" that afternoon about how dangerous fire can be, and how miraculous God truly is.

The stories that follow in this book will represent a few of the many lessons that I have learned throughout my childhood, adolescent and young adult years while living at (or associated with) my childhood address of 216 N. Lime. On my path to maturity, I experienced many situations that made grand impacts on my life. I label these situations as "Life Lessons." These events or Lessons worked to help shape my understanding of myself and the world around me.

Life lessons are the tools by which our characters are

formed. I believe that God takes every incident in our life and every decision we make, then weaves them into who we will become. If we are wise, we will use our "Life Lessons" as tools to help us manage our lives more effectively or as nuggets of wisdom to share with others along the way.

The knowledge that we gain each day of our lives prepares us for our future days to come. Our experiences or "Life Lessons" will work as steppingstones designed to give us the sure footing that we may need to maneuver to the next level or path of our lives.

"Life Lessons" can help define the boundaries that protect us from disasters, and they can also become the springboards that can propel us to greater heights. Some lessons may be harder to learn. But just like in school, if left unlearned, we most-times will have to repeat them.

Sadly, my childhood home at 216 N. Lime no longer physically stands. All that remains is a large empty, grassy lot guarded by an old chain linked fence. I have driven many times through my old neighborhood with my children and grandchildren and have shared many stories of the life I once lived there. Each time we visit that empty lot it spurs on a memory of another childhood adventure. My childhood home may be physically gone, but all the memories that were born there have continued to live on. I hope to continue those memories in this book. I have shared these stories and many others, with my family over the years, and now I hope to share them also with you. My desire is that you will be both entertained and inspired as you travel with me through "Lessons learned at 216."

New Bricks and Old Hula Hoops...

Carol (Age 3)

I don't remember much from my earliest childhood. My older sister Belinda has memories galore. She always tells us stories about when we use to live over on Lincoln Street and how she, my brother and I would play tag and jump rope outside in the front yard. Unfortunately, the Lincoln house is not in my memory at all. But I do remember the day we moved to our childhood home at 216 N. Lime.

I was three years old. I don't recall packing boxes or putting furniture in a truck. All I remember is standing on the brick sidewalk that traveled in front of our new home and looking through our swing set that straddled the sidewalk. I watched as my Mom and Dad scurried around the yard and in and out of the house. I remembered my Mom walking past me, then stopping to warn me not to go anywhere.

I must have had that look on my face that most toddlers have when thinking of doing something wrong. I just smiled and picked up my Hula Hoop lying on the grass next to the swing set. I tried to keep it suspended around my waist, but it was way too large to make the right contact around my hips, so it just made a quick swing around me once then fell straight to the ground.

My cousin Debbie was a master at Hula Hoop. She was a couple of years older than I was and tried to teach me the art of the hoop, but I never succeeded in getting mine to work. I just loved the "swooshing" sound it would make as it moved, so that alone would keep me entertained for some time.

How my journey began that day is somewhat of a mystery. At some point between watching everyone working to move us into our new home and desperately trying to make that hula hoop work, I became fascinated by the individual bricks in the sidewalk. It happened so quickly. It began with just one step at a time. I stepped on a straight brick, then a sideways brick. Next, a dark brick, and then a light brick, short bricks and then longer bricks, bricks stamped with numbers and bricks engraved with words. Before I knew it, I was down the block and around the corner. When I finally looked up, I realized that I wasn't home anymore.

There was not one thing that looked familiar to me because I had never been on that part of the sidewalk before. I don't know why I didn't just turn around. Instead, I kept walking, with my beloved hula hoop in my hand dragging faithfully behind me. All that my three-year-old mind could think was, "Where is Momma, and why had she disappeared?" I turned at the next corner, hoping that the red brick sidewalk would show me the way back home. I saw people moving around their yards and setting on their porches, all of them were looking at me, but none of them were my Momma.

About halfway down the block, I burst into a loud sob while calling my mother's name. "Momma...Momma! I want my Momma!" Soon one of the neighbors approached and asked what my name was and where I lived. Of course, I could not tell them where I lived, because I didn't know. All I knew was that I lived by the brick sidewalk that looked like the one on which I was walking.

The nice lady grabbed my hand and told me she would walk with me to help find my mother. So we followed the sidewalk hand in hand; her, me, and my Hula Hoop. We rounded one corner and still no Momma. We turned the next corner and then I heard it, my Mom calling my name! "Carol? Carol?"... It was the most beautiful sound I thought I would ever hear. My mother was looking for me! I looked down the sidewalk in front of me and there it was, my swing set, straddling the walkway just like it had been earlier.

I looked at my rescuer and exclaimed: "That's where I live!" The lady gently released my hand, and I ran swiftly down the sidewalk to meet my mother who had just stepped between the swings. I'm sure she was as happy to see me as I was to see her.

I was handed over to my worried parents' safe at home again, while my mother gained a new best friend in the neighborhood.

Even today, I am fascinated by the neighborhoods that still have the old brick sidewalks and streets. There is something nostalgic about their appearance. I believe they remind me of a much simpler time in my life when all that mattered was finding my way home.

Lesson Learned…"Stay in the moment and keep your head up!"
Unfortunately, I would have to learn this lesson repeatedly.

> *Isaiah 41:10* **fear not, for I am with you; be not dismayed,**
> **for I am your God; I will strengthen you, I will help**
> **you, I will uphold you with my righteous right hand.**

Daddy's Home

No Lesson. Just a Memory.

Daddy (Otis Bruce Jr.)

It is 3:00 p.m., and I am busting through my front door, racing my siblings to the sidewalk screaming in unison, "Daddy's home!" I wanted to be one of the first to reach him to get our daily "Muscle Ride."

Daddy would emerge from the car with a huge smile on his face and greet us with his usual, "Hey Chickens!" I'm not sure why he called us "Chickens." Maybe it was because he grew up on a farm? All I knew was that it made us feel special when he said it. As Daddy reached us, he would pull back the short-cuffed sleeves of his perfectly creased and pressed work uniform then curl up his arms to allow two and sometimes three of us to take the free daily ride. I remember feeling the strength of his solid hard biceps as I clutched on and felt my small feet leave the ground. Up and down, we would go. No carnival ride could ever replace the joy we got from these daily rides. This was my Daddy, and I believed he was the strongest man in the world. I knew that if anything terrible happened, my Daddy would be there to make it right. He was my hero, my provider, my security, and my rock.

Daddy worked two jobs. One at the VA Hospital and the other at the State Hospital. At least once a month, Daddy would present us with a gift from one of his jobs. Each of us would be handed a crisp, clean empty cigar box. We treasured those boxes. I especially loved the sweet aroma that was captured in each box. My cigar boxes would be transformed into a host of wonderful things, like a secret hiding place in the bottom of my pajama drawer or the treasure chest for our Pirate games. One box became a collection box for all the cool rocks and bottle caps I found while treasure hunting in our neighborhood. Others would be fixed with cloth handles to become a suitcase for my baby dolls. Still, some became a gift box for homemade Christmas and birthday surprises for my parents, a pencil box for school, and a crayon and paint box for home. Each month I waited for my fragrant container and planned a new life for its existence. Although I have many childhood memories, this one is the most cherished.

I know now that my father had to have been tired from an exhausting day of work, but he still took the time to smile at us and greet us in a loving way. It took just a few minutes to give us our "Muscle Ride" each day, but the impact has lasted a lifetime.

Upon the Rooftop

(The Santa Caper)

Belinda, Wayne, Santa, Cheryl, Carol

Raindrops on roses

And whiskers on kittens

Bright copper kettles and warm woolen mittens

Brown paper packages tied up with strings

These are a few of my favorite things.

This song always reminded me of the melodies and surprise of Christmas. It ranked high up alongside "Jingle Bells, White Christmas, Up on the Roof Top" and many more seasonal favorites. Christmas, to me, was all about favorite things. Christmas was magical; it was the only time of the year when you were permitted to even imagine and dream about getting all your heart's desires.

It seemed that everybody everywhere joined together in celebrating the most spectacular Holiday of the year. It did not matter what religion or race that you belonged. Everywhere you went, people were smiling and singing and greeting each other with a hearty "Merry Christmas!" It was as if a special Angel was dispatched the same time every year to sprinkled "Happy Dust" on everyone.

The season would kick into full gear the weekend after Thanksgiving. The city's main street, Kansas Avenue, would birth its yearly decoration of the most beautiful ornate garland that was woven with bright colorful Christmas lights. The garland spun from one side of the street to the other at each intersection. In the middle of each garland hung one of Santa's reindeer, with the reindeer's name boldly printed on their collars. My brother and sisters and I always had a contest to see who could remember the reindeer names by heart. Of course, we all knew which one was Rudolph.

It seemed like the whole town came out on that weekend to witness the ceremonial switching on of the Kansas Avenue Christmas lights and to watch the Annual Christmas Parade. The parade featured dancing snowmen and elves, horses, cars, and trucks decorated and adorned with holiday cheer. The last and best part of the parade was always a sleigh that contained a robust Santa Claus waving happily and tossing candy to all the children lining the street. It was Christmas time, and everyone and everything glowed during this time of the year.

After the festivities had ended we would hurry home and Daddy would go to the shed out back to retrieve the box that contained the sleeping aluminum Christmas tree and ceremonially set the box in the middle of the dining room floor. Daddy had purchased an artificial aluminum tree a few years earlier because it was safer than the fire hazard that the real trees presented. I missed the fresh smell of pine that had become part of Christmas, but the benefit was that we didn't have to sweep up pine needles every day.

Momma would be the one to untie the thick white ropes that held the tree safely in its box, and then she would extract the center pole of the tree and attach it to its footing. She would then remove each sparkling branch from its long paper sleeve and arrange them in groups on the floor according to their length. The lengths were identified by a color painted on the end of each rod. It was always the kid's job to construct the tree. Each branch was to be inserted into staggered slanted holes in the pole, beginning with the long limbs on the bottom and ending with the smaller at the top. It was a beautiful tree with sparkling silver fibers that caught the reflection of every light in the room.

Momma would place her fragile glass ornaments on the tree first, carefully attaching them securely on the tips of each branch. Then it was our time to fill in the rest of the tree with our collections of school made ornaments, glittered pinecones, aluminum stars, and colorful paper chain garland. It wasn't recommended to string lights on the aluminum tree because the wires could cause a fire. So, our parents purchased a rotating light of colors to shine on the tree, which caused the colors to dance cheerfully through the branches.

My mother loved Christmas. For her, it was the most wonderful time of the year. Her excitement spilled over into us as she transformed our home into a festive wonderland. Decorations would be everywhere. On the doors, on the walls, in the windows, across doorways, and on tabletops throughout the house.

Every year Momma would go to Sears and JC Penney's and obtain the most coveted item of the year...The Giant Toy Books! We would set for hours turning from page to page, claiming all the things we thought we wanted. Momma would sit and watch and listen, and somehow, she was able to decipher from our chatter what each of us might wish to have, even though most times we didn't even know what to pick.

Momma was what you would call an expert gift finder. I remember many years later when I would become a teenager that my sister Belinda and I wanted the extremely popular Maxi Coats. Most girls were wearing a traditional wool coat fashioned in a Maxi length. But our mother found for us, the most amazing, beautifully unique Maxi Coats ever! They were white, fake fur with heavy satin linings. No one in Topeka had one. Only my sister and me! I still even remember the sweet smell of the coat and how it felt as its warmth snuggled perfectly around my body. It had an oversized furry collar that wrapped around my neck and ears, blocking the coldest of winds that tried to get in. I felt royal and loved and, oh, so very special. I don't know where Momma found those coats, but they were the one gift that I would never forget.

We believed (like most kids) that the one real way to get what you wanted for Christmas was to talk to Santa himself. But for me, most times, these trips would prove to be useless. I would have in my mind exactly what I wanted for Christmas, but as soon as I sat on Santa's lap, all my thoughts would dissolve into a forgetful puddle on my tongue. Momma would just laugh at me and say, "Don't worry, Santa already knows." And somehow, he did! Because every Christmas morning, I would find that incredibly special gift under our tree. On this particular Christmas, I wanted a Chatty Cathy doll. You just pulled a string at the back of her neck, and she would say several different things like, "Tell me a Story" and "I love you." I just could not wait to talk to her and tell her that I loved her too!

Christmas Eve had finally come. Everyone worked together to do their chores to help get the house ready for the guest who would be coming over for Christmas Dinner. Some had the task of sweeping and mopping floors, while others had to wash the woodwork and windows. Momma would be busy cutting onions and celery for the dressing and peeling sweet potatoes for pies and marsh mellow topped casseroles. There would also be pudding to stir on the stove to make coconut cream pies and water for noodles that would become the world's best macaroni and cheese. The turkey would be seasoned exactly right and covered with heavy aluminum foil, waiting for the last slot to go into the busy oven for the night. The smells were intoxicating. They always put merriment in our step as they mingled in the air like a fairy's dance with the melodic songs of Christmas playing on the turntable.

Before long, we had finished our chores, and Momma gave us the green light to go to bed. Christmas Eve was the only evening in the year that we would beg to go to bed. Because Christmas Eve was all about falling to sleep and waking up early! We understood that the sooner we went to sleep, the faster Christmas morning would come. But falling to sleep was no easy task. Momma would hear us giggling and talking then would yell up the stairs, "You better close your eyes and go to sleep if you want Santa to come!"

It was a well-known fact in our family that if Santa caught you awake when he arrived, that he would throw pepper in your eyes to keep you from seeing him. We had never actually experienced this, but we were not brave enough to test it either. So, we would tightly squeeze our eyes closed as we laid wide awake trying our best to fall asleep while wondering what amazing goodies Santa would bring. Every so often, Momma would yell up the stairs warning us again about the penalty of being caught awake.

Finally, one by one, we all began to fall asleep. Just as I started to drift off into dreamland, I heard it! At first, it sounded like a thump on the roof. I shook it off and reasoned that it must have been an icicle falling from the tree or maybe a squirrel running across the gutters. I rolled over and tried to fall back to sleep. Then, there came what sounded like heavy footsteps on the roof above our beds. This time it was my brother Wayne who set up in the bed and whispered to me, "Did you hear that?" We both said in unison, "It's Santa!" We quickly slid down into our beds and pulled the warm winter covers over our heads. I heard my brother say, "Don't open your eyes...He's here!" I listened to the sounds of packages rustling under the tree in the room below us. There was no talking, just movement. Part of me wanted to jump up and look through the floor vent in our Parents room across the hall, so that I could just get a glimpse of the real Santa. But the thought of pepper in my eyes kept me snuggled in my bed. A few hours later, we awakened to our mother calling up the stairs, telling us that Santa had come and it was time to come down.

We all jumped out of our beds and began screaming with excitement. We descended the stairs surrounded by the arousing smells of Christmas morning swirling through the air. We rounded the corner at the bottom of the steps and then stopped dead in our tracks. We were shocked to see the magical beauty of the once, almost empty room, that now contained not only our sparkling aluminum Christmas tree but presents upon presents everywhere! There were shiny new bicycles, baby dolls, trucks, and doll carriages. Our once empty red Christmas Stockings were bulging with apples, oranges, nuts, and our favorite ribbon candies. Santa had come. And he came in the most magical way! "That was him that we heard on the roof last night," I whispered to my brother.

It didn't take long for us to rip through the wrapped gifts and to also lay claims on the exposed presents that were placed around the room. Somehow, Santa knew what everyone wanted, even down to my Chatty Cathy doll. Next, it was clean up time. Everyone shared in the pick-up of all the torn and discarded wrapping paper that was thrown everywhere in the room. There would be no playing with new toys until we completed the cleanup. So, we began the quick march to the back of the house to put the paper in the trash cans. As we were walking through the family room, Daddy opened the front door to allow the sunlight in. As we passed him, we heard him say, "Hey… what is that in the snow? Our curiosity caused us to turn and quickly hurry to the door. But Momma got there first. She let out a little gasp, then she looked at Daddy and said, "Should we let them see it?" "Let us see what?" We squealed. Daddy looked at Momma and gave a little smirk and said, "It should be alright."

Our parents parted from the door as we hurried forward and pressed our little faces against the small panes of the glass door. There in the freshly fallen snow where several sets of hoof prints lined up perfectly in the snow! My brother and I threw our hands over our mouths to hold in our screams. "It was him… It was Santa!" "Those are prints from his reindeer. We heard Santa on the roof last night, but we didn't open our eyes!" Our excitement was contagious, which caused our other sisters to jump around with excitement also. Momma and Daddy joined in our excitement, and the topic of "I heard Santa on the roof last night" was shared with all our guests and cousins that day.

I will never forget that Christmas and have tried myself to re-create the magic of that spectacular Christmas Eve with my children. But I found that each child and each generation will have to discover the magic of Santa on their own.

Lesson Learned: Life can be magical if you only believe!

Getting Even

Wayne, Belinda, Carol, and Ringo

Growing up with an older brother and sister isn't always easy. They can be your protectors, or they can be your private bullies. The relationship between my brother Wayne and my sister Belinda combined both factors. We were what people called stair steps, which meant there was a one-year separation between each of us. At school, Belinda and Wayne were my protectors. If someone were being mean to me, all I had to do was run to Belinda or Wayne, and they would take care of the problem. But the tables turned when we went home. No longer would they be my protectors, but they would become my bullies. It seemed like I had to pay for all the good things they did for me at school by doing what they demanded at home, which meant sometimes taking the blame for something that they had done wrong. It wasn't like we hated or disliked each other; we loved each other a lot. It was just your usual sibling line up of authority.

I was much smaller than Belinda and Wayne and third in the lineup, so it didn't take much to take full advantage of me. Secretly I had always said that someday I would get even with them for some of the things that they had done. That day had finally come, and I, by accident, stumbled upon the perfect way to pay them back.

My day of redemption started off like any ordinary summer

afternoon. Daddy was at work, and Momma had company over to visit. It was my Grandma Reece and our two babysitters, Barbara and Louise, from across the street. We knew that whenever we had company over, we had to be on our absolute best behavior.

My revenge opportunity happened late that afternoon, right as the sun began to fade. Momma had just reminded Belinda and Wayne to feed our dog, Ringo before it got dark. Our dog Ringo was short and stout like a beagle and had white fur with large brown spots. He had been with the family for many years and ate just about everything that we ate, but his main entree was a can of lumpy "Strong heart Dogfood." The dog food container was covered with sky blue paper and featured a picture of a well-groomed brown and black German shepherd on the front. We could have chosen other dog foods to feed Ringo, but we wanted him to be like the healthy dog on the front of the Strong heart can. Once, I had the task of helping to feed Ringo but had gagged at the smell of the sticky dog food and the gross sound that the food made when extracting it from the can. So, I was somewhat curious when I saw Belinda and Wayne quickly pickup two spoons to go feed our dog.

Belinda and Wayne quickly exited through the squeaky wooden screen door at the back of the house, as I quietly tip toed behind them and squatted below one of the windows adjacent to the door attempting to find out what they were up to. As I reached my hiding place, I heard them giggling and tempting each other to "try it first." I then pulled myself up to peek through the mesh-covered window and was surprised to see first Belinda then Wayne stuff a spoonful of Ringo's dog food into their mouths! I threw my hand over my mouth as I said, "Yuck!" Then it hit me... I can now get even with them. I immediately jumped out of my hiding place and yelled, "OOOH, you're in trouble...I'm going to tell Momma!"

I then turned on my heels and darted through the house, yelling, "Momma, Momma, Belinda, and Wayne are eating dog food!" Momma responded with, "They're doing what?" I chanted again, "They're eating dog food!" I knew that this would surely get them in trouble, especially since we had company over. Momma motioned for me to sit on the couch with Grandma while she went to see for herself what was going on.

I felt victorious as I sat on the couch. I started to laugh softly and swing my small feet up and down, happily singing, "Belinda and Wayne are in trouble." I smiled as Momma marched the two of them through the living room with a switch in her hand and angrily directing them into the dining room. She then closed the green vinyl accordion door, which separated the dining room from the family room. I could hear her asking them why they had put the dog food in their mouths. Then I heard them crying as the switch began to cut through the air. I remember sitting next to Grandma smiling and giggling as their cries filled the air. Grandma then leaned over to me and whispered a warning to be quiet before I also got in trouble. I looked innocently up at Grandma and responded, "But Grandma, I didn't do anything."

Suddenly the Green accordion door folded open, and I heard Momma command, "Carol get in here!" I thought to myself, "Why is she calling me?" As I entered the room, Belinda and Wayne were standing there looking sad with tears flowing from their eyes. As Momma turned to close the door, their sadness turned to smiles as they looked at me, then back to sadness when Momma faced them again. I knew at that moment that I was in big trouble.

Momma began to question me about the dog food episode, saying that Belinda and Wayne admitted to putting the dog food in their mouths. They also reported that I too had tasted the dog food! I couldn't believe what I was hearing. "NO, I DIDN'T," I blurted out. "Smell my breath, Momma!" "I didn't do it!" Momma did not smell my breath but responded with, "Why would they lie about you if they admitted to doing it themselves?" My eyes began to swell with tears, and my chin began to quiver as I realized that Belinda and Wayne's fate was now becoming mine. As I readied for my punishment, I thought to myself... "Revenge isn't so sweet."

Lesson Learned... Romans 12:17-21

Never pay back evil for evil to anyone. Respect what is right in the sight of all men. If possible, so far as it depends on you, be at peace with all men. Never take your own revenge, beloved, but leave room for the wrath of God, for it is written, "VENGEANCE IS MINE, I WILL REPAY," Says the Lord.

The Forgotten
Girl Scout

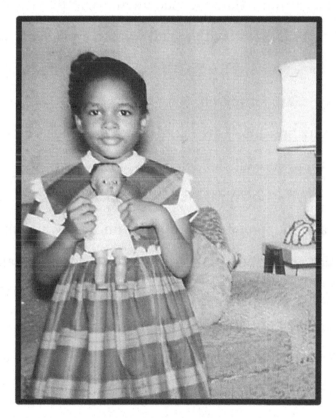

Carol (Age 7)

Summer break had ended, and the new school year was kicked off as always with the celebration of my Labor Day birthday. This year's birthday would be very special one because I would be turning seven and entering into the 2nd grade, which entitled me to join Girl Scouts! I had been waiting for this birthday for two years, because becoming a Girl Scout meant I could go to Girl Scout Camp! My sister Belinda and cousin Debbie, who were two years older than me, had been to camp twice already, and had eagerly shared with me all the fun and adventure that I had to look forward to. So, this year would be my year to experience camp for myself.

My induction into Girl Scouts was exciting. The girls in my age group were labeled as "Brownies" which was the first troop level in the organization. I remember going to Sears with Momma and shopping for my Brownie uniform which included a dress, hat, socks and a sash for my future badges. We also had to purchase a Brownie Girl Scout handbook that would teach me everything I needed to know about being a Brownie Scout.

My Brownie troop was scheduled to meet every Monday after school. Our meetings were held in one of the Annex classrooms behind my school (State Street Elementary) next to the playground. The Annex's were like small trailers that were made into classrooms.

I remember learning the Girl Scout Oath and eagerly scanning the pages in the handbook that instructed you how to earn badges. Some badges were earned as a group and some you had to earn on your own. I also remember that each person in the troop had to take turns bringing treats in the treat box. When it was my turn, I normally brought Tootsie Roll Pops or Momma would send homemade cookies. We were also taught songs like, "Make new friends" and "I got something in my pocket." I loved being a Brownie and looked forward to our meetings each week.

We had several Troop Leaders, but in my memory they are like the adult characters in the Charlie Brown cartoons. I know they were there, but for whatever reason I cannot remember anything about who they were or what they looked like.

Camp day had begun like any other school day. Classes had just dismissed and I and a few of my classmates came skipping out the school door laughing and talking about the days events. What was different that day was my Troop leader was standing out front and she was waving at me and calling me over to her car. She had this huge smile on her face and her eyes danced when she said to me, "Get in! We're going to Billard Park today for camp." Billard was a neighborhood park about ten blocks from the school and was used often by the many scouting troops in the area. I remember peering into the back seat of my troop leader's car and seeing several other members from my Brownie group who had also been corralled from the school yard.

Going to camp that day was a total surprise to me. We had talked about camp in our meetings, but no date had been set that I knew of. I remember thinking, "Momma didn't say anything about me going to camp today." But then I thought, "I'm sure it'll be ok? My only true hesitation with going was the question of how I was going to get my bike home. But that thought was quickly dismissed when the Troop Leader described to us all the fun we would experience playing on the toys, roasting hot dogs, making s'mores, and hiking the parks wooded paths. So, without any further thought, without talking to my brother and sister, and without permission from my parents, I jumped into the Troop Leaders car and was off to an afternoon of fun.

The outing proved to be as I imagined, and before long, I heard my Troop Leader calling us to go home. As I headed toward her car, I noticed that many of the other girl's parents were there to pick them up. I also noticed that outside the brightly lit park, it had gotten very dark! I remember the Troop Leader looking at me and a few of the other girls and questioning, "Where are your Parents?" A tinge of concern quickly grabbed me in the pit of my stomach as I realized that no one would be coming to pick me up, because no one knew I was at the park.

My Troop Leaders eyes were no longer dancing as they had been earlier, and her smile was now replaced with a questioning frown. I felt a whimper squeezing its way into my voice as I tried to explain my situation to her. The Troop Leader just gave me a long still look. At that moment I couldn't quite distinguish if it were compassion or disgust in her eyes when she finally agreed to take me home. But I assumed that she must have been tired just as I was from all the activities at the camp.

I sat quietly in the back seat by the far door listening to the gravel of the parking lot grinding below the tires as we pulled out of the park and onto the darkened street. Suddenly an even greater panic struck me. I had forgotten all about my bike at school, and I couldn't go home without my bike! I quickly turned to my Troop Leader and said, "Oh no, I have to go back to my school first to get my bicycle!" Her impatience with me this time was obvious as she let out a loud grunt. I really couldn't blame her, because not only was I in the car, but so were three other girls whose rides were late or not coming. So, my Troop Leader turned the car around and reluctantly drove me the ten blocks back to school to retrieve my bike.

When we arrived at the school, I jumped out of the car and told her that my bike was parked around back and that I would be right back. I made my way behind the school as quickly as my small legs would carry me. The once familiar school building appeared less friendly at night as its darkened windows mimicked hollow eyes watching my every move. I dashed through the shadows and pass the monkey bars on my path to retrieve my bike. As I rounded the old brick building's jagged corners, I suddenly stopped as a new horror became apparent. My bicycle was gone! "Oh no," I yelled, "Someone has stolen my bike!"

I quickly turned and retraced my steps back through the shadows and past all the dark windows to let my Troop Leader know what had happened. As I approached the front of the school building, I saw that the street was empty - My Troop Leader had left! How could she have left me? I told her that I would be right back. How was I supposed to get home in the dark? I looked around at the houses across the street, the playground, and the empty school building behind me, trying to figure out what to do next.

Suddenly, I remembered the Block Mother. Every block back then had what was called a "Block Mother" house. Each of these houses were marked with a window sign that said,

"Block Mother." These homes were assigned to be safe zones for children who were experiencing any troubles. I reasoned that I could go to the "Block Mothers" house at the end of the block and tell her that I needed to call my mom to come get me. So, I started running toward her house, but then I remembered that Momma had warned us not to speak to strangers. Earlier that year in our city, a little girl named Gladys Johnson had been kidnapped and murdered. Since I did not know the "Block Mother," I reasoned that she also would be classified as a stranger, which meant that I could not go to her. So, my only solution was to walk the thirteen blocks home, in the dark, by myself!

My face began to fill with tears as I dashed past familiar homes and favorite stores that now seemed to mock me in my flight. My terror intensified with each step as thoughts of kidnapers and loose dogs etched their way into my mind. I recall coming to the school light crossing in front of the Catholic school, which marked the halfway point to my home, when a car pulled to the curb and stopped.

A strange man opened the passenger door and whispered gently, "Get in little girl. I can take you home." As I looked into his eyes, all I could think was that he was the kidnaper who had killed Gladys. I began screaming, "Momma, Momma, help me!!!" With that, the man slammed his door and screeched off down the street.

I next remember running and crying through the crosswalk, then suddenly standing at my front door! I did not know how I got there. I just stood on the old wooden porch of my house, looking at my door and then looking franticly around my front yard. I began pounding my small fist uncontrollably on the door, crying and sobbing to get in, calling for my Momma. Before long the door flew open, and I fell into the protective arms of my mother.

After I had calmed down, my Mom told me that I must have run through some bushes because I had welt marks on my face. I couldn't remember nor find those bushes on my regular route to my home. I don't know if it was divine intervention or what. All I knew was that I felt frightened and alone, then suddenly, I was safe and sound at home.

I later found out that no one had stolen my bike, but that my brother and sister brought it home when they and Momma were out looking for me. I thought to myself, "Never again will I go somewhere without Momma's permission."

Lesson Learned: There's no value in

doing things the wrong way.

Psalms 121:7-8 The LORD will keep you from all harm-
he will watch over your life; the LORD will watch over
your coming and going both now and forevermore.

Whose Side Are You On?

Front: Wayne, Pam, Carol

Back: Louise, unknown, Barbara, Belinda

Children are sensitive beings. Especially when they feel that one sibling is getting preferential treatment over another.

There were four kids in our family at this point in my life: Belinda, the oldest, then Wayne, myself, and Pam, who was the youngest. I and my two older siblings were what are commonly called, "Stair Steps." This meant that there was only a year between each of us. Pam was fourth in line and was three years younger than myself. We all got along fine. We loved playing cowboy and Indians, school, house, and other childhood games.

On one day, Momma and Daddy had to leave and go shopping, so they called one of our babysitters, Barbara, to watch us. Barbara was the teenaged daughter of one of my mother's neighborhood friends who we called Ms. Willabell. Their family lived directly across the street from us, which was highly convenient for my parents. Whenever my parents needed to go somewhere, they would just make a quick call to Ms. Willabell's house and either Barbara or her sister Louise would come right over. Barbara was beautiful. She had a smooth dark-skinned completion and an even more beautiful youthful smile. She was about 15yrs old and was much taller than my mom, which didn't take much because Momma was only a few inches over 5 foot herself. Barbara was an excellent babysitter except for one small problem; she favored our little sister Pam.

She and her older sister Louise would always be doting over Pam and talked about how beautiful Pam was, how Pam's skin was a rich color brown like Barbara's and that she looked like one of the pretty black baby dolls in the store.

Now, even at our young ages of six, seven, and eight, we knew that usually, the baby of the family always got special treatment. So, it didn't upset us too much that Pam at age four was getting more attention than we were. We were accustomed to Barbara and Louise coming over and asking to take Pam to the corner store, and then bringing her back with a bag full of penny candy. And we restrained ourselves when Pam taunted and teased us with that candy. But this afternoon, we had decided that enough was enough.

The day with the babysitter began like any other day. Barbara would play hide and seek with us, push us on the swings, and sit with us to watch cartoons on the television. As I stated earlier, she was a good babysitter. The problem began with the cookie jar. Belinda wanted a cookie, so she got a chair and reached on top of the white metal cabinet in the kitchen to grab the container. When Barbara saw what she was doing, she quickly yelled for Belinda to get down and to leave the cookies alone. Wayne then asked why we couldn't have a cookie. Barbara replied, "Because you don't need one." I did not say a word because I figured that if she told Belinda and Wayne no, that meant no for everyone. Pam was sitting on the long brown couch at the end of the family room with Barbara, and we heard her ask, "Can I have a cookie?" Barbara looked at her, leaned over and hugged her and responded, "Of course you can have a cookie, Pam."

Our mouths flew open as we looked at each other, then at Barbara strolling over to the cabinet, reached into the cookie jar, extracted a cookie, and then lovingly hand it to Pam. As Pam took the cookie, she looked at us, laughed, and then returned to sit back to the couch with Barbara. At this point, Belinda, Wayne, and I became so angry we almost cried. It didn't matter that much when Barbara and her sister took Pam to the store for candy, but these were "Our" cookies, and it wasn't right to give them only to Pam!

It was Belinda's plan of revenge that we decided to follow. The idea was that when Barbara laid down to help Pam take a nap (as she most times did), we would sneak up on her and beat her up. Belinda gave Wayne and I each a duty. She would jump on Barbara's back to hold her down, Wayne would pinch her on her legs and arms, and I would pull her hair.

It didn't take long to put our plan into action. We waited in the playroom off the kitchen until we heard Pam get quiet, which meant that Barbara had put her to sleep, which also signified that she too may have fallen asleep. We slowly peeked around the corner to see if their eyes were closed, then quietly tiptoed through the long family room toward the sleeping victims. As we closed rank on our prey, Belinda let out the yell, "Let's Get Her," as she began to jump on Barbara's back. Wayne immediately started pinching her legs and arms, and I started pulling her hair. Barbara woke up screaming for us to stop, but we continued our attack. Pam had woken up also, and Belinda looked at her and growled, "Do you want some too?" Pam quickly shook her head no and ran to the front door and announced, "Momma's here. I'm going to tell on you!"

The three of us jumped off the babysitter and ran out the door to meet Momma and Daddy so that we could defend our actions. Barbara came running behind us, complaining to Momma about what we had done to her. After Momma got everyone quieted down, she listened to the story, then explained to Barbara that she was wrong to give Pam a cookie and not the rest of us. She then turned to Belinda, Wayne, and I and told us that we were also in trouble for jumping the babysitter and that we would be getting a whipping. We didn't care that we would get punished because we had effectively protected our turf.

Barbara and her sister Louise continued to be our babysitter for several more years without incident. We loved them both even though Pam continued to be their favorite. But, I do believe that Barbara realized that favoritism has its place.

Lesson Learned: Never stand in the way of a
kid and their cookie? Ok, this is better...

(1 Peter 3:9) Don't repay evil for evil. Don't retaliate with insults when people insult you. Instead, pay them back with a blessing. That is what God has called you to do, and he will grant you his blessing.

Sweet Discipline

"Sunday after Church with the Grandkids"
**Cheryl, Grandma, Belinda, Pam, Daryl,
Wayne, Carol, Tammy, Debbie**

The one day of the week that was always marked as special in our house was Sunday. It was the one morning of the week when the aroma of bacon and eggs filled the air to awaken us from the night's sleep. Suddenly there would be little bodies jumping from the beds and rushing downstairs to be the first to get cleaned and have breakfast. The first person that we would see upon entering the kitchen would be Momma standing over the stove cooking. Daddy would be sitting at the far end of the table reading the Sunday paper. He would surgically remove the comic section of the newspaper, making sure not to disturb the rest of the paper's flow. He then laid it neatly on the table to await the one who got dressed and ate breakfast first. Momma made it a point to get our clothes ready the night before to save time in the morning, so the actual race was to see who would get to the tub first.

Soon it would be time to leave for Sunday School. Daddy would call all of us to the kitchen, and we would eagerly gather around the table to get our offering for class and church. He must have saved all his quarters from the previous week because he would have a stack of three quarters on the table for each of us, one for class and two for the church.

As we picked up our precious piles of quarters, we secretly knew that at least one of the coins would not make it to the offering plate. That coin would buy candy from the corner grocery store by the church. I always wondered if they ever knew our secret or just trusted us on the honor system. On some Sundays, we lived up to their trust, but on most, we would exchange the small silver coin for a few minutes of sugary sweet delights!

Sunday School was a little bit scary to me when I was younger. Our church was located on the corner of 12th and Lane, and was appropriately named 12th Street Church of God. The Nursery and Primary classes were in the top back half of the church, and the only way to reach them was by climbing (what seemed to be at that time) a never-ending flight of stairs. I can remember that when I was in the nursery class that my teacher would smile and loudly greet us every Sunday with, "Good morning! Have a seat." Whoever had taken me to the class that day would let go of my hand and ease me into the room. I would immediately start crying, not because I was afraid of the teacher, but because I believed that I could never find my way back down those long stairs. My fears would subside somewhat as we started the lesson for the day, and they would completely disappear by the time my older sister and brother arrived back to get me at the end of class.

Several years had passed, and I was now a member of the

Primary class and the only scary thing about Sunday School was being asked to read aloud. Most people know the feeling. You realize that you will be next to read, but your heart is pounding so loudly in your ears that you can't concentrate on the words on the page. You only know that once the person before you has finished, you will have to begin. It wasn't that I couldn't read. It was just the fear of sounding dumb by mispronouncing a word.

Daddy worked on Sunday afternoons, so Momma usually stayed home to see him off. Neither one of them regularly attended church except for holidays, so our watcher at church would inevitably be Grandma, our Momma's mother. Grandma was very active in our church. She taught classes, was on the Deacon Board, and she sang in the choir, which meant that we got to sit all by ourselves on the back pew during church services.

I can still see Grandma marching in with the choir every Sunday morning singing, "We Are Soldiers in the Army." Their heads were held high and their faces were so intense that we teased that all they needed were helmets and a gun then they could be real soldiers. We didn't understand at our young age, that the battle they were singing about wasn't one fought against a foreign nation, but against foreign gods who tried to take the true God's place in our daily lives.

Neither Grandma's place in the choir nor her constant eye connection prevented us from cutting up and talking throughout the service. Nor did it keep us from eating the candy that we had bought at the corner store. The trick was to do these things without Grandma seeing us. Brother Stinson, (who seemed to be our "Personal" usher) would frequently come to us and say, "You Bruce kids better be quiet before I tell your Grandma." I don't know why he always singled us out as "The Bruce Kids", because our cousin Debbie was part of the commotion also. But Debbie always had a way of saying something and making us laugh while maintaining an innocent looking exterior.

We would quiet down for a little while, but soon start giggling and talking again when we thought no one was looking. Before long, we would get this uneasy feeling that someone was watching us. And sure enough, when we looked up in the choir stand, Grandma would be glaring at us, giving us that, "You better straighten up" warning with her face which verified that she had been observing our antics all along! After about two or three of these looks, Grandma would quietly dismiss herself from the choir and join us on the back pew. Whenever this happened, we knew that our disrespectful actions would be reported to Momma when we were returned home.

On one certain Sunday, Grandma joined us on the back row.

But, after church, when we had all loaded into her car, instead of giving us her usual soft lecture, she looked at us and said, "How about stopping to get some ice cream on the way home?" We were stunned at first but quickly and eagerly answered, "Yes!" So, before we got home, Grandma stopped by the Dairy Queen and treated us all to a soft vanilla ice cream cone. While we ate our ice cream, I whispered to my brother and sisters, "I think she forgot what we did at church today." We just smiled and continued to eat our creamy treats.

When we arrived home, Momma asked the usual question, "How were the kids today?" We all set confidently around the kitchen table, finishing our ice cream cones, knowing that Grandma would answer, "Oh, just fine." Unexpectedly, Grandma started telling all she had witnessed about our conduct in church service that morning. She did not leave anything out! She reported to Momma how disappointed she was in us that we choose to talk and eat in church and that Mr. Stinson had to quiet us several times during the service. Momma then got a stern look on her face and pointed her finger at us and said, "Wait until your grandma leaves!"

We were speechless, and all we could do was to stare at Grandma in disbelief. How could she betray us after buying us ice cream! Grandma then explained that she loved us and that it would not be right to let or behavior go unpunished. If she did, that would show that she did not care about our well-being. Somehow, we all understood what the ice cream meant. Grandma had demonstrated that discipline should be administered with a loving attitude, not out of anger and disgust.

Now that we are grown, we all still laugh about Grandma's "Sweet Discipline." Unknowingly she taught us all a valuable lesson that day on being better future parents. We learned that discipline is necessary for our development. However, discipline should always promote learning and growth, and should never belittle or destroy.

For this lesson, I say, thank you, and "I love you, Grandma!"

(Ephesians 6:4) And now a word to you parents. Don't keep on scolding and nagging your children, making them angry and resentful. Rather, bring them up with the loving discipline the Lord himself approves, with suggestions and godly advice.

A Reflection of Time

Carol (Age 8)

One of the many things that I loved during my childhood was going to school. At school, I could learn new things, but mainly I had the opportunity of being with my friends for most of the day. Like many kids, I felt that recess was the highlight of the school day, but the second-best part was lunchtime.

Back in the early 1960s, there wasn't such a thing as school lunches at our school. So, each year our parents would buy us a new metal lunch box to carry our lunches in. We preferred using the plain brown paper bag for lunches, but they didn't hold up well in wet or snowy weather.

For us, lunchtime meant Bologna and catsup sandwiches, Lay's Potato Chips, a piece of fruit and either a few cookies or a cupcake. Our school provided the lunch beverage, which was a small carton of the coldest, sweetest milk that I had ever tasted. Momma always gave us the flexibility to request what we wanted in our lunches, but on frigid day's she would back our lunch box with a thermos filled with vegetable soup along with our favorite sandwich.

There would be a few days, throughout the school year, when we wouldn't have enough time to pack our lunch for school, mainly because we had overslept. On those days, we would have to go home for lunch. Going home was okay for the kids that lived right down the street from the school, but some of us lived much farther away. Our house was precisely one mile away, so it was almost impossible to make it home, eat, and get back to school without being late. Because of this, Momma allowed us to ride our bikes to school on the mornings that we were running late. Riding bikes was fun because you could travel much faster than you could walk. It usually took about 15-20 minutes to walk home, but it would be half that time on our bikes.

Our parents had drilled into our heads, the rules of safe bike riding. We understood that if there were sidewalks, we would ride on them instead of in the street. We also knew to watch the corners for oncoming traffic and to always have me ride between my older brother and sister because I was the youngest.

I had two friends named Peter and Jimmy, who frequently walked home for lunch. They were brothers, but not biological brothers. Jimmy's family had adopted Peter, and the two had become inseparable.

My brother and sister and I had flown past Peter and Jimmy on our bikes, and I had disobediently taken the lead. I waved at the two boys as I passed them and yelled, "I'll see you back at school!" Their responses were somewhat garbled due to the speed at which I rode past them, so I turned my head to say,

"What?" while my bike continued forward. I saw their faces change as they began screaming something and pointing. I thought that they were impressed that I was able to ride my bike and talk to them simultaneously. Little did I know that they were trying to warn me that I was approaching "Danger!" Not far ahead of me was a huge Whelan's truck, parked by the curb.

Whelan's was a lumber company that transported large volumes of lumber on long, flatbed trucks. These trucks had enormous side mirrors that measured about 2ft tall and extended to the side of the truck about one foot. When I finally realized that Peter and Jimmy weren't yelling because my bike riding skills were so impressive, I heard Belinda and Wayne yelling, "Carol! Watch out!" My head seemed to turn in slow motion as I approached my impending fate. All I remember was seeing my reflection in the large side mirror of the Whelan's truck. It was quick, and it was painless. One moment it was sunlight and then the next, total darkness. Before I could think or react, a piece of my life was forever lost! The rest of this story is recalled only through the first-hand witness of my sister and brother:

They told me that as I turned my head forward, I hit the Whelan's truck's side mirror head-on. The impact was so hard that it sent my bike spiraling backward, knocking my sister and brother off their bikes. My body was airborne within the same motion of time, and I crashed headfirst onto the concrete pavement below me. The sound was immense, causing all the people who lived on that block to come running out of their houses. People were scurrying everywhere, each asking what they should do.

Several of them asked Belinda and Wayne if they wanted them to call an ambulance. (To this day, I still wonder what prompted them to inquire of an eight and nine-year-old their opinion as to if they should call an ambulance.) So, of course, their response to the question was, "No, she'll be alright." I can only reason that they said no because then was the age of Disney. We believed in happy endings, and that children could never be harmed. So, an ambulance was not called. I just lay motionlessly on the hard-concrete,

*unconscious of the world around me. Several
minutes later, my lifeless body began to move as
I tried in vain to struggle to my feet. They told
me I got up and then fell again several times
before I reached full consciousness.*

As I came to, I remember seeing a large group of people
standing around me. I began crying, and someone asked if my
head hurt. I looked at them and whimpered, "No, but my finger
does." With that, everyone sighed relief and decided that I was
okay. A few offered to drive us home, but Belinda and Wayne
declined, saying that we could walk the few blocks to our house.
Momma and Daddy had always taught us never to take rides
from strangers, so they must have decided that this situation
would be no different. So, the neighbors handed us our bikes
and sent us on our way. Belinda and Wayne's bikes were a little
scratched, but mine was not only scratched, but it had dents, a
flat tire, and a slightly twisted frame.

Momma was already out on the porch of our house when we
rounded the corner. She immediately asked, "What happened
to Carol!" Wayne and Belinda told the whole story about what
had happened, while Momma cleaned and bandaged my only

wound from the accident, my cut finger. It was amazing! I didn't have a headache or even a knot on my head. How could I have fallen so hard and not been seriously injured?

Momma then looked at us with tears in her eyes and told us that about the time we should have been leaving the school on our bikes, she had an awful feeling that I was going to be badly hurt. She said that she immediately began praying to God that he would protect me and keep me safe. To this day, I believe that Momma's prayer saved my life. How else could a seven-year-old child survive such a tragic fall and emerge with such a small injury? The accident didn't keep me from riding my bike again, but it did teach me that riding a bike is an enormous responsibility that requires your full attention.

Lesson Learned..."Stay in the moment and keep your head up!" Sound familiar?

(Luke 4:10) for it is written, 'He will command His angels concerning you to guard you,'

Along the Way...

No Lesson. Just a Memory.

I know many of us had listened to your Parents' or Grandparents' stories about how, when they were children, they had to walk a mile to school. It is hard to believe with all the transportation conveniences that we have today that those stories were true. But my childhood home was precisely 13 blocks from our elementary school, which equaled one mile.

My siblings and I didn't grow-up in the country. We grew up right here in Topeka, KS in the neighborhood called Oakland. There were a couple of schools just a few blocks from where we lived, but they were Catholic schools. And since we weren't Catholic, we were enrolled to attend the closes public school which was called State Street Elementary.

Our Dad left for work early each morning, and our mom was a non-driver, which left us to walk that mile every day, be it sunshine, rain or snow! You might say that we lived the Postman's creed. On occasion, when it was too cold or wet, Momma would call the Yellow Cab to drop us at school. I don't remember "not going to school" because of snow or cold; I'm sure there were some days. Then again, everyone attended their neighborhood school, so no one stood on corners in the cold waiting for school buses to come.

Along the walk, we would find unique things like, cool rocks; fuzzy caterpillars; money; and most thrilling, a cocoon attached to a low- hanging branch. We would break off the twig that contained the cocoon and take it to our teacher at school. That way, the whole class could have the opportunity to watch it mature and eventually emerge as a beautiful butterfly. We would always set it free, but it was just thrilling to witness how a fuzzy caterpillar could evolve into a graceful butterfly.

I recall that rainy days called for raincoats, rain hats, and galoshes. Galoshes were rubber boots that we wore over our shoes. They call them garden boots nowadays. Snowy day attire included those same rubber boots and thick, full-bodied, or two-piece, hooded snowsuits. The ensemble was completed with thick mittens, a hat, and a Vaseline covered face to protect our skin from the cold air.

The one-piece snowsuits were very unforgiving. You pretty much had to walk with your arms extended to your sides like the little boy in the movie "A Christmas Story." It was almost impossible to get back up on your feet if you were to fall. I remember sliding and falling on the icy sidewalks several times and begging my brother and sister to help me up. Most times, they quickly grabbed each of my hands and pulled me to my feet. But sometimes they would laugh as I struggled to get up off the ground, before helping me.

We lived in a true neighborhood. The positive thing about

that was, there were four stores along our 13-block trek, and all the storekeepers knew our parents and us. The first stop was called "Eakes," the second was a hardware store, and the last was Tilton's and Blaylock Drugs. We knew that if it got too cold or wet outside, we were welcome to stop at any of the stores to warm up a bit before continuing our walk to school. Sometimes one of them would treat us with a small cup of Hot Chocolate and rub our cold little hands before sending us back out on our route.

Once we made it to school, it became undressing time, which consisted of disrobing from all our outerwear. The school Principal designated a large part of the front hall for all the kids to peel out of their outer coats, snowsuits, and boots before going into the classrooms. There was always a group of smiling teachers on hand to help. The hardest part of the process was leaning against the wall while trying to dislodge your shoe out of the cold, wet rubber boots. Most kids could kick out of their boots without a problem, but one of my shoes would always get stuck halfway inside. During the struggle to free it, my foot would pop out of my shoe with my sock in tow. Then, I would invariably step into a waiting puddle of cold water on the floor. A teacher would hurry to my rescue, only to play tug-of-war also with my shoe that was stuck in my boot. I just never mastered the art of getting both of my feet out with both shoes on.

Just about everyone had snow gear or heavy coats and gloves to weather the cold. We loved the cold weather and would play for hours in the snow. If we lost a glove, our Mother would double up some of Daddy's old work socks and slide them on our hands.

Back then it seemed that every house had a snowman, and when we had an extra heavy snowfall, we would build snow forts at the foot of our porch and have snowball fights with the neighborhood kids. The clothing we wore to endure the cold could be purchased at any department store. But today, most times, you would find these things in a specialty store that sells items for skiing.

Times have changed since I was a child. My children lived part of my childhood for a very short while. But, eventually, they joined the "now common" group of kids who step out of warm houses, into warm vehicles, and then are dropped at the front door of their school. Some have never seen a caterpillar or the birth of a butterfly. But I along with other parents of this age, have the assurance that when we drop our children off at school, that they have arrived safely. But with that comfort comes a loss of adventure, "Along the way!"

Vacation
(The Vanishing Fish Mystery...)

Grandpa (Otis Bruce Sr.)

It was the last day of school and everyone had cleared and cleaned their desk. The classroom trash can was filled to the brim with crumpled papers, broken crayons, discarded paint tins and pencils that were now only a little larger than the smudged erasers on their ends. The anticipation of summer break was contagious and the classroom buzzed with conversations about summer plans. The teacher tried her best to retain order in the class as everyone fidgeted in their seats, eagerly waiting for the final bell. This time of year always excited me, because in our home, the onset of summer meant one thing: Vacation!

My father grew up in Texarkana, Arkansas, and most of his brothers and his sister still lived there. So every summer, when other kids in our classes were visiting Mount Rushmore, Pikes Peaks, Yellowstone Park and Disney land, we packed our bags and headed to Arkansas!

As the day approached for us to leave, the excitement would become almost unbearable. There were many preparations to be made, such as selecting groceries for the trip, buying new short sets and tennis shoes for all us kids, meticulously packing suitcases and bags, and a complete head to toe check-up for the car.

The journey getting to Arkansas would almost be as much fun as the visit itself. It normally took about 12 hours to reach

Texarkana. But a few years earlier, Daddy's brother (Uncle Leroy) who also lived in Topeka, had found a new route that shaved four hours off the trip, which made the journey only 8 hours now.

There was something about going on vacation that made everything appear magical. We loved watching the sun-kissed scenery roll past as the warm air blew through the opened windows and caressed our faces. The fresh smells of the open road and the rhythmic roar of the tires seemed to enhance the trip's excitement. Our favorite part of the route were the tall, jagged, rocky hills that periodically framed the sides of the passing highway. It always felt as though we were driving through a topless cave.

Momma always made the trip fun with songs, road-games, and of course, fried chicken sandwiches and Oreo cookies. Daddy did his part by getting us there safely and ignoring our touchy moments when we complained that someone was sitting too close to the other, or that one person was looking at the other too long.

Our excitement mounted as we got closer to our destination and the conversation would then turn to "Momma, are we there yet?" No matter how far away we were, Momma's reply would always be, "Its right around the corner!" So, for each bend of the road the question would repeat itself, and Momma's patent answer would be the same. We soon realized that if we would force ourselves to fall asleep that the time to get there appeared to pass much faster. Before long, I would hear Momma calling us to wake up to see the Billboard welcoming us to Texarkana, Arkansas. Screams of excitement would fill the car with the anticipation of soon seeing relatives and friends again.

Daddy's relatives lived on the outskirts of Texarkana in the county division called Mandeville. Mandeville's characteristics at that time, were red dirt roads, horses, cows, pastures, and outhouses. We always felt like the city mice coming to visit the country mice, but as children, these qualities spelled "Adventure!" As we entered Mandeville's boundaries, Daddy would begin honking the car horn and relatives would emerge from the old wood-framed county homes that lined the dusty red roads. Daddy would say, "There's your Aunt so and so, and your Uncle whoever." We never remembered their names because there were so many of them. However, when we saw our favorite cousins, who were daddy's brother V.J.'s kids, we would wave wildly and scream out the window, "We'll be over soon."

Our first stop was always Grandpa's house. Grandpa would hear our car honking from blocks away, and as we rounded the corner, he would be standing on the porch with his hands on his hips and a grand smile on his face, waiting for us as we pulled into his drive. We always knew that our family was welcome in his home.

The gravel would still be crackling beneath the car tires as we began to flip up the door locks. Momma and Daddy would tell us to "Hold your horses" and to wait until the car stopped. When the car finally came to a stop, we would jump out and race over to be the first to give a great big hug to Grandpa and his wife, Ms. Veatrice. We had instructions to call her "Ms. Veatrice" because she was Grandpa's second wife and not our Daddy's Mother.

Oh how we loved Grandpa! Grandpa was always full of stories and we loved how his lips would pop after each word. We were captivated by the sound of his voice. Grandpa's farm was spectacular. He had cows, horses, geese, chickens, roosters and a couple of grumpy bulls that we were warned never to tease. One year Grandpa took us out to the barn to watch him milk his cow. After he was finished he brought the bucket of milk into the kitchen and poured a little into each of our glasses to taste. I remember taking a sip and saying "Yuck!" The milk was warm, thick and sour. It was nothing like the milk our parents purchased at the store. There was always something new to experience on Grandpa's farm. The one thing we didn't like about the farm was the outhouse. There was no running water on Grandpa's farm, so if you needed to go to the restroom you would have to visit the outhouse. The outhouse was horrible. There were always flies and wasp guarding the doors and stool inside. The outhouse set in the middle of the pasture where the cows and bulls grazed, so we had to time it just right to run to the outhouse when they weren't looking.

Grandpa also drove the county school bus and we had the privilege of traveling with him several mornings as he picked up kids for Summer School classes. One year he actually enrolled us in class. I remember riding on the bus and singing with the other kids, "I have ten green bottles sitting on the wall, if one fell over and accidentally fall, I'd have nine green bottles sitting on the wall." The song would continue until there were no green bottles sitting on the wall! The other song was simply called "The Name Song." In that song you would sing words that rhymed with your name.

After arriving, we helped our parents unpack the luggage from the trailer, then tried to decide which of the day's activities we would indulge ourselves in first. Would it be visiting our cousins, chasing the chickens, or fishing?

Chasing the chickens and geese had become a vacation

highlight. But Ms. Veatrice had already warned us not to chase the chickens because it upset them, and they wouldn't be able to lay as many eggs. We didn't mess with the geese much, because we had learned by experience that when we chased them, they would turn and chase us back! So, we decided that after visiting our cousins we would go fishing. Unfortunately, it was already late afternoon when we arrived, so we only had time to visit with our cousins.

Our meeting place was always in front of Uncle V.J. and Aunt Minnie's house under the large shade tree. It was there that we talked with our cousins and caught up on the year's events and plotted our adventures for the week. Uncle V.J. and Daddy were tag team brothers. For several years everytime Daddy would have a baby, so would Uncle V.J.! The results were that all of us had a cousin to match up with, except for Belinda, she was the oldest of all of us. My brother Wayne and Mirvus; me and Virginia; my sister Pam and Glenda; My sister Cheryl and Jackie. Years later Uncle V.J. and Aunt Minnie would out number us in kids, but Daddy and Momma ran a very close second. When I reflect back, I realize that most of our idle time was spent under that large shade tree. We spent hours each day under that tree, talking, dreaming, laughing, and teasing the younger cousins and siblings. It didn't matter if it were scorching hot, we stayed under that tree. Only the occasional rain would run us in.

We also had a friend who lived down the road from our cousins, named Reginald, who joined us in our planning. Reginald was one of those people who would be your friend one day and your enemy the next, but we still classified him as our friend because, most of the time, he was a lot of fun to hang around.

We had made plans the next day to go fishing but our cousins weren't able to go because they had chores to do at home. So, reluctantly, we decided to go alone. The fishing trip started as planned. Daddy first took us down to the fish bait store to pick out the biggest, juiciest earthworms for our hooks. He then dug our bamboo fishing poles out of the back of the trailer. Daddy checked all the lines and made sure that the hooks were secured tightly on the line, then issued my sister Belinda, my brother Wayne and myself our poles. We laid the poles over our shoulders like Huckleberry Finn and begin our adventure across the field to the fishing pond.

The fishing pond was on Grandpa's property and set quite a ways from his house, but not so far that our parents couldn't see us from the porch. Tall narrow pine trees were stationed around the pond, which provided a cool shade on a hot summer day. We had to be cautious as we crossed the fields because Grandpa owned a lot of cows, and as everyone knows, cows do not use the outhouse. We also had to keep an eye out for snakes, and to make sure that we didn't do anything to disturb the bull that was casually watching us nearby. As we were traveling through the field, we heard someone calling us from across the pastures. We turned to see Reginald running through the tall pine trees to join us. He had his pole also, but no bait. We were hesitant in letting him use our bait, but then agreed that we would share some of our worms with him.

When we reached the pond, we each took a worm and tightly wove its wiggling body onto our hook so that the fish would not be able to get it off quickly. The fish were hungry and biting that day, and we ended up with a bucket of about 7 or 8 large fish. Grandpa had already told us that if we caught enough fish that he would clean them and cook them for dinner that night. We felt proud that we would be able to provide the main course of the meal. We talked about how everyone at the table would be commenting on how delicious the fish were and how we were good fishermen.

Unfortunately, Reginald did not catch any fish that day. He kept saying that he was on the wrong side of the pond, or that we had given him the skinny worms. We all laughed at him and teased him by saying that he didn't catch any fish because the fish didn't like him! He soon tired of our taunting and decided that he was going home. With that we all left the pond and ran back to the house to show Grandpa our catch. Grandpa was surprised that we had done so well and instructed us to leave the fish on the porch while we cleaned ourselves up, then we could watch as he cleaned the fish.

Since Grandpa didn't have running water in his house, cleaning up meant that we had to retrieve water from the well. I remember that the well water was always cold and sweet. We didn't mind using the well because we liked to crank the handle and watch the bucket that was attached to the end of the rope, emerge from the deep dark depths of the ground. In the mornings, Ms. Veatrice would pull several buckets of water from the well, and heat the water in large pots on the stove. She would then pour the water into a large metal tub on the back porch so that we could take our baths. It was so much more adventurous than turning water on in our tub at home and waiting for it to fill.

As we were cleaning up, we heard Grandpa calling from the back of the house, asking us where we had put the fish. We gave each other a puzzled look then ran to the back porch to see what was up. We found the bucket setting on the ground next to the porch, but all our fish were gone! Grandpa assumed that a wild animal or a cat had come and eaten the fish, but we told grandpa that we believed that our "friend" Reginald had stolen the fish instead. We reasoned that if an animal had taken the fish, the bucket would be toppled over. But the bucket was sitting up straight with all the water still in it! Grandpa agreed that it was a little strange but warned us never to accuse anyone without first talking to them and seeking out the facts. So, we decided to take a trip across the pastures and pay our friend a little visit.

On the way to Reginald's house, my brother talked about how he would beat Reginald up if he had taken our fish. My sister agreed that she would also help. As we approached Reginald's house, we smelled the pleasant aroma of freshly fried fish in the air! We knew for sure now that Reginald had taken our fish because he had not caught anything that day! We quietly crept up to the side of his house and peeked through the rusted screen of the open window and saw him and his Grandmother sitting at the table eating our fish!

Our first instinct was to knock on the door and tell his Grandmother what he had done. But before we could react, we heard his Grandmother say that she was so glad that he had caught the fish because they would not have had anything to eat that evening if he hadn't. About that time, Reginald looked toward the window and saw us looking in. We looked at him, but didn't say anything; instead we quietly slipped away from the window and hurried back to grandpa's house.

We felt terrible that we had wanted to beat-up Reginald for taking the fish. We also felt bad that we had teased him about not catching any fish. The fishing trip, for us, was just something fun to do, but to Reginald, it was a matter of going to bed hungry or not. It had never occurred to us that there were families that did not have enough food to eat. Our parents were always able to present a meal to us, and we knew that fish or no fish, we would still have a big meal that night.

When we arrived back at Grandpa's house, we told him about what had happened. He explained to us that Reginald's Grandmother didn't have a lot of money to buy food for her family most days and that the neighbors help when they can.

Later that evening Reginald came over to apologize, and we told him not to worry about it. We saw Reginald differently after that day. We didn't pity him; we respected him for doing what he had to do to help his Grandmother.

Lesson Learned: A person should not judge another person's action without first looking at all the facts.

> *(Luke 6:37) "Do not judge, and you will not be judged. Do not condemn, and you will not be condemned. Forgive, and you will be forgiven."*

The Cellar

Carol, Cheryl, and Pam

It was springtime the weather had become stormy as it typically does during that time of year. I was nine years old and had graduated to the level of part-time babysitter for my younger sisters Pam and Cheryl. Part time babysitter meant that I could watch them while Momma ran quick errands where she was gone for no longer than an hour. My instructions were to stay inside, watch T.V. and to keep the doors locked. No one was allowed into the house when she was gone unless they had a key to get in. I remember one time our Uncle Leroy (Daddy's Brother) came to the house when our parents were gone. He knocked to get in and we looked at him through the window and said, "No! Momma and Daddy said not to open the door when they are not home." My Uncle Leroy go so mad he stormed to the car and drove away. Later he told our parents what happened, and my Parent's laughed and said, "They were only doing what we taught them to do." He couldn't argue with that.

I'm not sure how I got stuck alone that day watching my two little sisters by myself. It normally would be a team effort that included my older siblings. Momma had to run an errand somewhere that included taking my older brother and sister, Wayne and Belinda, with her. The weather started to change quickly that afternoon. At first I noticed that the sun wasn't shinning as brightly through the windows as it had been earlier. Next I heard the distant rumbling of thunder as the storm began to brew. I had calmly instructed my sisters to ignore the sounds of the thunder and to watch the TV, but my untrained ears could tell that the storm was heightening outside the closed door of the house. Soon we heard a louder clap of thunder then next the reflection of a bolt of lightning flashing outside the windows. Suddenly the wind began to whip ferociously around the house, while the heavy raindrops fell loudly on the roof. I instructed my sisters to remain seated while I went to the door to see what was going on outside. I was trying to be brave for my sisters, but the truth was that the increasing sounds of the storm were making me very nervous also.

I had never liked storms because there always came with them the possibility of something more dangerous; Tornadoes! As I looked out the door, I remembered Momma would watch the clouds' movement to determine how hard the wind was blowing. She would also notice the changing colors of the sky. She observed that when the sky was gray to dark gray, it usually meant we were in a bad thunderstorm. But if the sky had a yellowish or greenish color that often indicated the possibility of a tornado. I noticed on this day, the sky was an eerie yellow, and the clouds seemed to roll like angry waves across the sky.

Our family had a basic routine that we followed in the event of a Tornado. If the tornado whistles blew, Momma would take us across the street to Ms. Ella's house, to take cover in her basement. We lived in an older neighborhood, so most of the homes, like ours, had dirt-floored cellars. We did not like going to our cellar because it was always dark, damp, and musty, which meant big spiders and large water bugs would be waiting for us. Mrs. Ella and her husband had a full finished basement in their home, so they had invited all the neighbors to come to their house any time there was a threat of tornadoes.

Ms. Ella and her husband were what you would call "good neighbors." During the spring and summer months, you would always find Ms. Ella and her husband working together in their flower and vegetable gardens. They always seemed to be happy. I never heard them argue or even raise their voices at each other.

One year after returning from vacation, we noticed that my cat was missing. We looked everywhere for the cat but to no avail. Early the next morning, Ms. Ella came to our house and told Momma that my cat had been hit and killed by a car. She explained that she knew how much I loved the cat, so she had her husband wrap it up and buried it in her flower garden. She took me over to her yard and showed me where she had buried my cat, and I cried as I hugged her. I was sad that my cat was dead but happy that Mrs. Ella's flowers would always surround it.

The weather now had gone past a thunderstorm and was edging into tornadic weather. I turned and looked at my sisters and said, "I think it's time to go over to Ms. Ella's house." Pam and Cheryl immediately started to whine about having to go out into the storm. I told them to get their jackets and put them over their heads to help keep them dry. I then opened the door and readied for our flight through the yard and across the street. As we stepped out onto our porch, a low yawning sound began to feel the air. I recognized it immediately as the tornado siren!

Almost simultaneously came large frozen hailstones and an even stronger wind, which forced us back into the house. Pam and Cheryl were crying now and asking what we were going to do. I evaluated the situation quickly then openly decided, "We will have to go to the cellar." A look of horror crossed my sister's faces, as they belted out, "NOT THE CELLAR!" I tried to explain to them as clearly as I could, the gravity of our situation, as the house seemed to sway around us. I told them that we had to go to the cellar because it was too late to go to Ms. Ella's. What happened next was almost comical had it not been in a time of emergency. Both sisters dropped to the floor then latched their bodies onto my legs as their attempt to stop me from taking them to the cellar!

I started screaming at them to let go, as I struggled to drag each foot forward, through the kitchen, and toward the cellar door located in the floor of the back porch. All the while I was trying unsuccessfully to pry them off of my legs. With each step I took, my sisters kept pleading, "Carol, please don't make us go down there, we'll be good, we'll do anything you want, just don't make us go down there!" It seemed that it took us forever to make it to the cellar door.

When we finally reached the back-porch, the storm had gotten so bad that the windows had begun to bow in and out from the pressure of the wind. When I bent down to grab the cellar door latch, my human leaches - like magnets - jumped off my legs and onto the top of the cellar door as a means of preventing me from lifting it opening. I couldn't believe they were doing this! The windows were about to be shattered and blown in on us by the wind, yet my sister's where jumping up and down on the very door that could lead us to safety; all the while screaming, "I don't want to die!" With all the strength I could muster, I grabbed both of them, pulled them off the door, opened the cellar, and forced them down the stairs. None of us wanted to go all the way to the dirt floor, so we sat on the bottom three steps and closed the door above our heads. I prayed that nothing would happen to our house and that no spiders or bugs would attack us on the stairs. Soon the all-clear sounded, and we emerged from our musty fortress, un-bugged and unharmed.

As I reflect on that day, I am still awed by the reactions of my sisters. It puzzles me as to why they would choose to face the present danger of the storm rather than to face the perceived fear of "The Cellar."

Lesson Learned: Fear of the unknown can be greater than knowledge.

"I learned that courage was not the absence of fear, but the triumph over it. The brave man is not he who does not feel afraid, but he who conquers that fear." Nelson Mandela

---

Bath Time!

Pam, Cheryl, Wayne, Carol, and Belinda

Torturing the younger siblings in a family setting is quite common. It is sort of like a rite of passage. As you are elevated up the family ladder with the birth of a new baby, it became your right to become the enforcer over the younger sibling. When I was the youngest, my older siblings Belinda and Wayne tortured me often. Their favorite thing would be to lock me in the little house.

The little house was a small house on our property where we stored stuff like the large walking dolls that Grandma gave us for Christmas each year. There were also boxes of old clothes, tools, and bicycles. We hated the walking dolls. They were big and scary, and thanks to the Twilight Zone Movies, we believed they came alive at night. So, we would systematically destroy them every year, but then every Christmas Grandma would gift us with another.

I would always be the last to put my bike into the little house. I knew that Belinda and Wayne planned for me to go last, but they promised that they would not lock me in. And for some unknown reason, I would believe them. As soon as I entered the little house, they would slam the door shut and hold it closed. Then they would yell through the door that the dolls were going to come alive and get me. I, in return, would start screaming and crying for them to let me out. After a few minutes, they would open the door and tell me that I was a crybaby then run into the house laughing.

Several years had passed since then, and two new sisters were now added to the family. I had graduated to the status of one of the older siblings, and we had two more little sisters, Pam and Cheryl, to torture.

Pam and Cheryl were always an easy scare. It didn't take much to get them going. With Belinda, Wayne, and I working together, we could creatively come up with something original. We wisely choose our opportune time to enact our tortures, usually when Momma had gone shopping, and Daddy was at work. One of our favorite scares were turning out the lights and hiding from the younger sisters in the house. Then we would jump out from behind the doors and couches and say "Boo" when they searched the rooms to find us. Of course, they would scream, and we would laugh at the success of the scare.

Another scare was to wait until it was dark and force them to go outside to feed our dog, Ringo. Once we had convinced them to go, we would lock them out and start screaming, "Run, run. The Boogie Man is coming!" Pam and Cheryl would start screaming and beating on the door to get in, while we laughed so hard that our sides began to hurt. We would then let them in and tell them not to tell Momma because we were only playing. Many of these incidents would never get reported to our parents because we would somehow convince them not to tell. Cheryl was younger than Pam, so many times she traveled with Momma, which sometimes left Pam to be the victim alone.

One night we devised the ultimate scare for Pam. Earlier that week, we had seen a movie, which starred Betty Davis, called The Nanny. It was about a little girl who had drowned in a bathtub of water, then came back to haunt the woman she believed had caused her drowning. Today this movie probably would not be that scary, but back then, this type of story was very frightening. We were all afraid to go to sleep for several nights following the film, but that did not stop us from re-enacting it on Pam.

Pam had a bad habit of waiting until the last minute to take her evening bath, so we used her habit as an opportunity to play out our sibling scare. Momma, as usual, had left for a few hours and put Belinda in charge since she was the oldest. We planned to wait until the sun went down and then remind Pam to take her bath. We knew that she would procrastinate until the last minute to do it. So, all evening, we kept saying, "Pam, you better take your bath before Momma gets home!" We always knew when Momma was coming because you could hear the brakes of our old red station wagon squealing from about two blocks away. Its sound always allowed us enough time to get things straight before she got to the house.

Well, Pam kept putting off her bath, and we took advantage of her predictability. While she was busy doing other things, we slipped one of those life-size walking dolls into the bathroom and laid it under the bathwater to look like the little girl in the movie. After we had set up the scene, we walked into the family room and said, "Pam, listen. Do you hear that? Momma's coming!" Of course, we were lying, but Pam fell for it anyway. Pam was a swift runner, and she used all her natural speed as she rounded the corner of the family room door, through the kitchen and into the bathroom. Just as she reached the old claw foot tub, she saw the doll lying under the water. We heard her scream and then bolt out of the bathroom as Belinda, Wayne, and I fell to the floor, laughing.

She didn't cry, but she did have tears in her eyes when she threatened to tell. We told her that we were sorry and begged her not to say anything, and Of course, she agreed, which set us up for the second part of the scare.

Two of us consoled her, allowing the other one to go back into the bathroom to stand the doll up by the tub. The plan was to make it appear alive and that it had come out of the bathtub on its own. Before long, Pam had forgotten about the initial scare of that evening; all we had to do was let her watch her favorite shows to make her happy again. When we saw that Pam was all smiles, we began to plot on how and when we would get her back into the bathroom.

It wasn't long before our opportunity arrived. As we sat and watched the TV, we began to hear the all too familiar, "screech, screech," of the old red station wagon brakes. We all looked at Pam, who knew that she was in trouble for not taking her bath, and said, "You better hurry up, Momma's here." Pam again broke out into her fast-paced run. She rounded the family room door and dashed through the kitchen. She threw open the door of the now dark bathroom, flicked on the light, only to be encountered by the life-sized doll waiting for her with outstretched arms! We all had followed behind her flight to see what would happen. We were not disappointed when Pam let out a horrifying screech and came flying out of the bathroom backward, smashing into the refrigerator and crumbling into a mass of tears on the floor.

Our laughter was now uncontrollable as Momma entered the door with Cheryl in tow. I don't think I need to say what happened to us, but today Pam has a beautiful gray streak of hair growing on the left side of her head. The doctors said that it was a result of medication that she took for an allergic reaction to Cherries a few years later. But Pam attributes it to our ultimate scare when she was nine years old.

Lesson Learned? I don't know, maybe not to have fun at another person's expense? Yeah, that's it!

Wishing for Rainbows

(The Tornadoes Wrath, June 8, 1966)

Carol (Age 10)

"We're the Red

We're the Blue

We Belong to the VBS

We Love to sing Praises to our King

In the house of God

As we work and Sing

We're the Red

We're the Blue

We'll be on our way

We're as happy as can be

We're so happy you can see

We belong to the VBS!"

Each year, at the end of every Vacation Bible School day, the Red and Blue song would ring loudly throughout our small church, Church of God 12th and Lane. The battle was always between the nursery/Primary classes and the pre-teen/teenage classes. Every time the younger group would win because the older kids thought they were "too cool" and "too grown" to participate. The prize (usually a piece of butterscotch candy or a tootsie roll) was motivation enough for my friends and myself to sing as loud as possible. The final reward was that the winning group would be the leaders as we left the building.

It was 1966, and I was ten and a half years old. It was essential to count that half-year because each year added to the double digits brought about new privileges. There is something special about turning 10. You somehow hit a level of young maturity when suddenly you become concerned about how your hair looks and if your clothes fit a certain way. You're not ready to look for a boyfriend or girlfriend, but you are keenly aware of who is cute and who your secret crush is. But in the same breath, you are still fascinated with playing with your dolls and other treasured toys. That one year added to your age, which took you from a single number to doubles, sets off a whirlwind of changes.

I remember the pianist positioning herself at the piano as her fingers began to play the all familiar Red and Blue song. All the students stood up, with the younger and older kids on opposite sides of the sanctuary. For reasons unknown, on that day, the older kids decided that they, and not the younger kids, would win the battle. I remember taking a deep breath and, along with the others in my primary class, and began to belt out the words of the song, "We're the Red, We're the Blue...We belong to the VBS!" The older kids were belting out the song also and our voices united in a harmony that practically shook the entire building! The result was that the older kids accomplished an overwhelming win. I remember the VBS teachers smiling and clapping, so proud that everyone had finally participated. The older kids collected their hard-fought-for prize candy along with the prestigious honor of leading everyone out of the church. The older kids sneered at our younger group as if to say, "See, we could have beaten you whenever we wanted!"

My sister Belinda was with the older kids and had the privilege of leading the line, but when she opened the door to exit the church, she saw something strange and alarming and flung her arms out, stopping everyone in their tracks. The sky was no longer the standard summer blue that it had been when we entered the church that evening. It was now very dark and colored an eerie greenish-yellow, and the atmosphere was very still and heavy. Not a leaf rustled on the branches of the many trees lining the neighborhood street. Even to the untrained eye of a child, you could sense danger!

Belinda immediately yelled, "Tornado!" Then I heard the teachers' gasp as they hurriedly pulled us from the doors and quickly ushered us all down the stairs into the basement. I remember hearing one of the Teachers comment that if the younger group had won, they would have been outside running around playing before noticing the danger. Almost immediately, we heard heavy raindrops, then the gushing down of rain that drenched the outside grounds. Next, we heard hard balls of hail pounding the roof and the sidewalks outside. Following the noise was a roaring wind like I had never heard before.

The teachers gathered us all to one side of the basement and instructed us to sit on the floor. The phone in the church's kitchen began ringing, and I heard someone ask the caller, "Is it on the Ground?" Immediately the teachers started yelling, "Stay on the floor and cover your heads; a tornado is heading this way!" The announcement instigated screams and crying from the children, and some asking, "Are we going to die?"

Then all the teachers began praying. They prayed spontaneous, earthmoving, and spirit-filled prayers. The moment became too much for me. I, along with my brother Wayne, my sister Belinda, and my cousin Debbie, decided that if we were going to die, we wanted to see what was about to kill us. So, we said to each other, "Let's look out the window." We quickly popped to our feet and pulled back the curtain of the window that was right above our heads. As we looked out, we saw shreds of paper, small limbs, trash cans, and leaves suspended in the air and swirling around the church! Without hesitation, our voices echoed with the phrase, "It's the tornado!!" The teachers yelled at us to sit down and we flopped to the floor, covered our heads, and prayed that the church would be okay.

Minutes later, the roaring storm subsided, and for us, it was all over. Reports of the storm's devastation and path echoed from a radio that one of the teachers found in the church office. The newsman announced that the city was still under attack from the storm, and the tornado was now heading towards East Topeka. The reporter continued with a warning that everyone was to stay in your shelters and take cover immediately.

Our home was in Northeast Topeka in the Oakland area, so we asked Momma if the tornado would hit our house. She tried to assure us that everything would be fine and that even if our home were to be destroyed, that God would take care of everything. We all looked at each other, then I said, "If the tornado destroys our bikes, we can get new ones!" So, my brother and sister and I decided that if God takes care of all things that He would know that our bikes were old. So, if we prayed for Him to take our bikes in the storm and leave our house, He would do it. So, we hurried to a corner of the basement, and together, we prayed for God to let the tornado take the "Little House" where or bikes were stored, so that we could get new ones.

It seemed like we had been in that basement for hours

before the city confirmed that it was safe to go home. My Grandmother tried to convince my Mom to stay at her house, located just a few blocks from the church. She reasoned that the streets would be too dangerous to travel with all the downed trees and power lines on our route home. But Momma decided that it should be safe to make the journey home.

Before leaving, Momma called our Dad who was at work at the V.A. Hospital, to see if everything was okay with him. His encounter with the tornado still sends chills through me today. My Dad said that he and the staff were trying to get all the patients to a safe area when they spotted the tornado forming on the horizon. First, it was just a swirling of winds and small debris; then, it began to morph into a gigantic white, then black, angry cloud right before their eyes. He said that it was moving straight towards the hospital and was growing larger and stronger with each rotation as it destroyed homes and decimated trees and power lines that were innocently in its path. My Dad said everyone knew that there was no way of escaping the tornados rage. So the entire staff just stood paralyzed in their steps. He said that what happened next was nothing short of a miracle. One minute the tornado was practically on top of them; the next moment, it suddenly turned and went a completely different direction, missing the hospital altogether.

I recall hearing my mother re-telling the story to the other ladies at the church. And I thought to myself, "God must have set up some kind of invisible barrier in front of Daddy's hospital to make it turn away." And if God can do that, I knew that He could also get rid of our bikes! I suddenly was excited to get home to see if God had answered our prayers.

The ride home was awful. It had gotten extremely dark outside, so Momma had to be extra careful as she slowly drove through the streets. She decided that the safest route would be to go straight down 10th street. I have never witnessed the destruction of a war zone, but I'm sure it resembled what Topeka looked like that evening. The streets were empty but for the exception of a lone car here and there, and there was an eerie quietness that had settled over the city. Many of the buildings and houses lining our route were missing windows with roofing and debris scattered throughout the yards. Tree limbs and trees were down everywhere, and the trees that remained standing were stripped naked of their leaves and now presented broken jagged limbs.

I remember Momma driving around downed power lines that lay here and there in the streets. But nothing prepared us for what we saw at the corner of 10th and Kansas. The multi-storied building on one corner was no longer standing but now lay in a heap of jumbled and crushed bricks. The other building adjacent to it across the street was still intact, but was now leaning and swaying from side to side each time the restless wind blew. Momma quickly rushed past the corner in hopes that the building wouldn't fall as we were trying to pass by. It wasn't long until we were cresting the Branner Bridge and entering our neighborhood. We were relieved to know that we were almost home, and before long we would know if God had granted our petition for new bikes.

It was still raining, and the distant sounds of thunder were still quietly vibrating in the atmosphere. Occasionally, we would witness a soft crackle of lighting in the distance. As our car slowly rounded the corner of our street, we saw our house. "It's still there!" We squealed. We crossed our fingers, hoping to see that the "Little House" was gone. The Little House was positioned to the back and side of our property so it couldn't be seen until you entered the yard. Momma slowly steered the car into our driveway, allowing the lights from the car to illuminate our yard. And to our dismay, the Little House was still there-untouched! Our bikes remained just as we had left them. Our prayers had not been answered! I saw the relief on Mamma's face that our home had escaped the storm. Many homes in the city and community were destroyed or damaged that day, but our house and our bikes were spared.

A couple of hours later, Daddy arrived home and took a survey outside to document any damages. He called us to the back door and asked us to look out into the yard to see if we saw anything missing. The backyard was dimly lit by the back porch light. Our swing set was still there, and the large tree behind the house was still intact. At first, everything looked the same. But then suddenly we saw it. The small shed that use to house our toys, (but now was Daddy's tool shed) was gone! No roof, no wood slates, no tools, no lawn mower...nothing was left! All our mountain climbing adventures were over. No more climbing onto its roof and jumping to the ground. The tornado did visit our home that frightful evening. It reached down behind our house, away from our bikes, and took the shed. All I could say was, "It took the wrong one!"

Today I understand the blessing in the storm. Our daily shelter had been left intact, while many people that year had to start their lives over. They had become instantly homeless, not knowing how to replace it all. They had lost their homes and all the irreplaceable memories of pictures and family heirlooms, and some had lost their very lives.

So, the now grown-up Carol recognizes the miracle of that day. I reflect with awe at how the tornado switched paths and spared the lives of my father, his coworkers, and all the patients at the V.A. Hospital. Also, how that same tornado hovered above our small church but decided not to drop its deadly hand and destroy the children and teachers huddled in the basement. I marvel at how it then skipped through my neighborhood, totally missing our home and our bicycles but seamlessly removing the shed that stood just yards away. Yes, our family was blessed beyond measure that day while the children loudly sang, "We're the Red, We're the Blue, We'll be on our way. We're as happy as can be, We're so happy you can see, We belong to the VBS".

Lesson Learned: Selfish Prayers never work! God is all-knowing and works to protect us, even in our ignorance.

Busted on Branner Bridge

My Brother Wayne (12yrs old)

> *"You can ride your bike around the*
>
> *block, but don't go any further!"*

I can still hear Daddy's words echoing through the air. The only problem was that Wayne was now a pre-teen, and he had already decided that he would break the rules.

Wayne had just received a sleek new bicycle for his birthday. It was red with skinny tires, which made it ride more smoothly and faster than our older big, bulky bikes. He had raced everybody in the neighborhood that day and won! The race participants would line up on their bikes in the street side by side with one foot on the ground; then, one of us who was not in the race would say, "Get ready, Get set.... Go!" Everyone in the race would take off, pumping their pedals as fast and hard as they could, racing the full length of the block. Wayne had defeated everyone with his slick new bike, and now it was time for the ultimate challenge...Branner Bridge!

Branner Bridge was more of a neighborhood bridge. It was a thorough fair connecting our neighborhood, called Oakland, with the rest of the city. The only hours of the day that the traffic was heavy were around 7:00 or 8:00 am, and 4:00 pm, which was the time that the Santa Fe workers went to and got off work.

Several boys at school had bragged about how they could ride their bikes, full speed, down Branner Bridge, and Wayne had decided that he would not be left behind. None of us knew that Wayne had already planned the time when he would take his challenge, which would be early afternoon. I don't remember the exact time he executed his plan; I would guess right after lunch, between 1:00 or 2:00 pm. We usually shared all our secrets, but this time we found out about his plan second hand.

Wayne began circling the block in front of our house and behind our home several times that afternoon. His slim, red, shiny bike sparkled in the summer sunlight. He would ride fast, then slow, and sometimes without any hands. Soon it came time to implement his secret plan. After his last ride around the block, he pulled his bike into our driveway where Daddy was cleaning the car and asked if he could go to "Pete's" to buy some candy. I'm sure there was a conversation about if he had any money or not, and he must had because Daddy agreed to let him go. So, Wayne jumped on his new sleek, red bicycle and disappeared down the block.

"Pete's" was a small grocery store located a couple of blocks from our home. It wasn't unusual for us to ask to visit the store. We would enter its doors at least once every day. Momma always sent us there for milk, bread, and other needs. But what we liked most was that they had the best selection of penny candy in the world. There was a glass display cabinet behind the register that housed a vast assortment of sugary sweets, and most of it only cost one cent each. My favorites were a coconut candy shaped like a slice of watermelon, banana Now or Laters, tootsie rolls, and black licorice whips. All it took to acquire a full bag of candy was a pop bottle, that we could redeem at Pete's for ten cents a bottle. If we found a penny in the yard or on the street, we could get a treat at Pete's. But Wayne's trip to Pete's that day wasn't for the candy; it was a cover for his plan to get to Branner Bridge that was only a block away.

Daddy was just finishing cleaning the windows on the car when we began to hear an unfamiliar click, clonk, clank echoing from down the block. Then we noticed the sound of a person moaning loudly as if they were in deep pain. Daddy stopped wiping the windows and walked out to the sidewalk. He looked down the block to see what or who was making the strange sounds, and we followed quickly behind him. That's when we saw him. It was Wayne, pulling and dragging his once new, sleek, shinning red bicycle! The bike was noticeably destroyed! The frame was twisted and mangled, and the front tire was no longer attached but was now an oval shape in Wayne's hand. His clothes weren't torn, but he was very dusty from head to toe.

Daddy just stood there staring, not sure what to say at first. As Wayne entered the yard, Daddy angrily asked, "What happened to you?" My sisters and I immediately knew what had happened. Wayne had challenged the bridge and lost! And now he was in big trouble!! But Wayne's reply to daddy's question was not what we expected at all. He looked Daddy straight in his eyes and, while rubbing his dust-covered head, replied, "Who are you? Where am I? "Who am I? Daddy was startled by his reply and began yelling, "Boy, you know who you are! Don't act crazy with me!" But Wayne maintained the confused look on his face as he continued his questions.

My sisters and I got scared then because we initially thought he was faking, but now we didn't know what to think. We ran inside and told Momma, "Wayne's hurt and doesn't know who he is!" Momma hurried outside to find Daddy and Wayne conversing about who he was. It was evident that Daddy was shaken with Wayne's situation. So, it didn't take long for Momma to convince Daddy that they should take him to the hospital. So, they loaded Wayne into the back seat of the newly cleaned car and headed to the hospital. We waved as the car pulled away with Wayne looking aimlessly out the car window, rubbing his head, and starring into the sky.

Luckily, the doctors didn't identify anything wrong with

Wayne. When he finally arrived back at home, he miraculously began to get his memory back. He started looking around with a thrilled expression on his face saying, "Hey, I know where I am now!" He looked at me and our sister and declared, "I know who you are, you're Carol, and you're Belinda. Then he looked down at our dog and said, "Hey, Ringo...I know you too!"

None of us, including our parents, ever really knew if Wayne was acting or if he genuinely had been hurt. The topic of Wayne's strange day was never discussed again. Even today, I'll ask him what happened that day. But he only gives a slight smile and looks away. All we know is that he never tried the Branner Bridge challenge again...I think?

Lesson learned: Some things in life will forever be a mystery!

Sticks and Stones

Carol (Age 11)

Every child has a teacher who they admire because of the impact they had on their lives; that individual teacher who encouraged them to be the best picture of themselves. My special teacher would be my 6th Grade teacher, Mrs. Dreiling.

Each school year would begin with a Parent-Teacher meeting. Our parents would be invited to the school to get the list of needed school supplies and the name of the teacher that had been assigned to teach their student. I recall waiting at home, anticipating which teacher I would get for 6th grade. All my friends were hoping to get Mr. Sanders. Mr. Sanders was known as the fun teacher in the building. He had a way of persuading his students to enjoy learning.

On the other hand, I wanted Mrs. Dreiling because my sister Belinda had her for a teacher in the 6th grade, and she thought she was an excellent teacher. I liked the way Mrs. Dreiling stood with her class in the hall. She was tall and regal, always holding her head high. Her classes were known to stand at attention, not rigid just proud and orderly. Mr. Sander's class would be shifting around and giggling at funny faces he might be making at them while Mrs. Dreiling governed her kids with quiet control. Mrs. Dreiling had high expectations for every student. She never accepted "no" or "I can't" from me or anyone else in her class. She forced us to learn even when we thought we couldn't. There was security in how Mrs. Dreiling handled her class and carried herself, and I wanted to be just like her.

By the time I reached Sixth Grade, children were beginning to understand the meaning and power of discriminatory words, and I would be called some of those words periodically throughout my Sixth-Grade year. There were only about ten African American students at our school, so it didn't take long to figure out that these new words were developed to be used only against us. Most teachers would just look at me and turn their heads when I reported the name-calling while on the playground, or they would quote, "Sticks and Stones," suggesting that I should just ignore the name-callers. Mrs. Dreiling, however, took a different approach.

One afternoon my class was out for recess and was engaged in a game of kickball. I was always one of the first picks on a team because I was known to kick the ball far, even though I was a slow runner. My friend Paula was on the opposite team that day, though we usually got picked together. My team was up with the bases loaded, but the other team was ahead in points. It was my time to kick, and everyone on my team was yelling, "Kick it hard, Carol!" The pitcher rolled the ball, and I kicked it with all my might, and the ball went flying across the field, allowing all the runners on base to score, and putting our team ahead.

I had made it to 2nd base when I heard the recess bell ring to go in. I ran over to my friend Paula to walk inside with her as my team was celebrating. When I reached her, she looked at me angrily, then using one of her newly acquired hateful words, said, "Leave me alone, "N!" I usually just shook it off and walked away, but the words were especially hurtful this time because they were coming from my friend! I retaliated by slapping her and yelling at her to not call me that name, then I turned and ran back to class.

After returning to class, I heard Paula crying in the hall and telling Mrs. Dreiling that I had hit her. Mrs. Dreiling called me out to the hallway, and with a stern look, demanded to know my side of the story. I just knew that I was in big trouble and would be sent to the Principals office, especially since I had been repeatedly instructed to just walk away when someone called me a nasty name.

I was in tears by now and bravely told Mrs. Dreiling precisely what happened. "Paula called me an "N" because I kicked the winning run in the game, so I got mad and slapped her!" Mrs. Dreiling looked at me in astonishment because she knew that I was not one who would hit or fight. She instantly turned to

Paula. Instead of hugging her and sending her back into the class, Mrs. Dreiling scolded her about respect and friendship, then demanded that she apologize for hurting my feelings.

Mrs. Dreiling turned back to me and, in her firm reassuring tone, told me that even though it's wrong to hit others, it's never right for people to call me hurtful names just because of the color of my skin. She went on to say that I was a kind and smart girl and should always be proud of who I was.

From that point forward, Mrs. Dreiling became my hero. She taught me that it was alright to stand up for myself, even when others seemed not to care. She never allowed me to give up on learning, and in the end, I learned not to give up on myself!

Lesson Learned: Words many times
are more painful than stones.

(Proverbs 18:21) Death and life are
in the power of the tongue...

Yes Ma'am & Yes Sir...

No Lesson. Just a Memory.

Front: Cheryl, Pam, Carol, Wayne

Back: Belinda, Momma

Traveling to the south as a kid opened a whole new world of communicating. The niceties of how we communicate in Kansas, drastically changed when we crossed the Arkansas border.

Our parents had always taught us to respect our elders. We were to give direct eye contact and to respond with the word "Yes" when addressed by an adult. But, when we crossed over into Arkansas (where my father's family lived), we came face to face with a much different cultural training. Whenever my cousins were speaking to adults, they were required to humbly respond with "Yes Sir" or "Yes Ma'am." It didn't matter if they were responding to their parents, an adult relative, the next-door neighbor, or the clerk at the grocery store. The appropriate response should begin and end with the "Yes Sirs" or "Yes Ma'am's." Of course, we thought it was funny, and as we got older and more aware of our cultural history, we thought it to be repulsive.

We had heard these words echoed on T.V. movies as slaves spoke to their masters. And we had always wondered why our cousins had not ever rebelled against being forced to continue using the phrases. Our parents never required us to use the "Yes Sirs" and "Yes Ma'am's." So, whenever we visited our families down south, we would openly flaunt our freedom to express only "Yes." We quickly announced to Aunts and Uncles that Momma said that we did not have to respond the way that they did! Surprisingly, none of the relatives ever made a big to-do out of our response. They understood that certain things were different in other parts of the country. We never disrespected them; we just were raised differently. When I think about it, I don't know why Daddy never enforced his up bring on us. Because as soon as we were around his family, he naturally reverted to using the "Yes Sirs" and "Yes Ma'am's" as though he had never ceased.

Years have passed, and I, like my Mom, have passed on the "Yes" tradition to my children. Sometimes they would deviate, and "Yes" would become "Yeah," which brought about a scolding, but the tradition continued. Even as adults, when my siblings and I reminisced about growing up, we always laugh about our escape from the "Yes Sirs" and the "Yes Ma'am's."

But then one day, out of the blue, as my wisdom grew, my perception began to change. I began to recognize the power of the words that I had shunned all my life. I realized that these words were not a symbol of submission or shame, but actually, they were an indicator of respect! Somehow those words built an internal image of character inside of the user that permeated through their pores and reached out to others, thus causing the receiver to feel good about themselves.

I began to hear the words echoing within the ranks of our military and spoken as a courtesy between friends. Had I missed out on a treasure that could have enriched my life? I began to wonder what doors have been closed to me simply because I had refused to express the magic "Yes Sirs" and "Yes Ma'am's."

Today I am on the receiving side of the once scoffed at terms, and I see myself softening my position and granting requests most often to those who use the magic words. I understand the power of full respect now and even wish that I had learned the secret earlier in my life. It's too late to teach my kids. But I do plan to pass the knowledge to them so that they can instill it into their children. There is an old saying that says, "You can't teach an old dog new tricks." My response is, "Yes Sir," "You're right!"

A Change is Gonna Come...

Within most family structures, the younger siblings in the family tend to get more privileges that the first of the clan. Our family was no different from any other in this respect. I learned very quickly that there would be certain privileges extended to the younger siblings of the family that, we at their age, would not even dream of enjoying. We were like trailblazers. Our parents perfected their parenting skills on us and then used their newly honed skills on the next in line.

We grew up in a majority Spanish neighborhood and many of the kids in our area attended catholic schools. But we were enrolled at the area elementary school named State Street. There were only about eight African American students at our school at that time, and the rest were Caucasians and a few Spanish. The racial balance of the school didn't matter to us when we were younger, but when we graduated to Jr. High and High School, our ethnic differences became very noticeable.

I remember when I was about twelve years old when my good friend Patricia introduced me to "Soul" music. My sister Belinda and I, at the time, were hooked on the other popular groups like "The Monkeys" and "Paul Revere and the Raiders." Patricia, who was also one of the few black kids at our school, had been introduced to the Jackson Five, the Temptations, and Marvin Gaye and she wanted to share her new bounty of information with me. It wasn't like we hadn't ever heard soul music before; we had always listened to Momma and Daddy's old records, but their music had a much different sound than the music Patricia was listening to. I had not realized how much music could shape your world until that day.

As I began to listen to this music, my world slowly began to transform. It was at that point when I realized that I was missing something valuable in my life, which was a deeper knowledge of my heritage. I don't blame Mom and Dad for denying us such a crucial part of our development. I now understand that they were merely trying to shelter us from the ugliness of this world. But in their trying, we were stripped of our ethnic awareness.

It wasn't unusual for my sister's and I to tie bath towels around our heads in a pretense of having long straight hair like our friends at school. We saw them as beautiful and yearned for our hair to look like theirs. So once a month, Momma would take us to her hair dresser to have our hair washed, dried and pressed so that our hair would hang in shinny long locks like our friends. But now, James Brown was shouting a song titled, "Say it Loud! I'm black and I'm Proud!" And suddenly we saw the beauty in our brown skin and kinky hair, and in turn took down our braided ponytails so that we could wear our natural

"Afro's." I began to gain a different understanding of my life. It was empowering, beautiful and exciting. I began to see me!

I will never forget the day that Martin Luther King Jr. was murdered. I showed up to my Junior High school the next day as normal but was met at the door by the Principal and then rushed into his office. He informed me that I could not come to school that day because "They" would burn down the school! I was completely confused as to what he was talking about. I asked, "Who is They? And what does it have to do with me?" He responded that because Martin Luther King Jr. had been killed, the city was under siege and Black Activist groups were burning buildings in the city. He went on to say that if they saw me they would think I was being forced to be there and would burn down the school. My next question was, "Who is Martin Luther King Jr.?" I had absolutely no clue who he was or why the city was supposedly being burned. With that, the Principal called my parents and demanded that they come pick me up. But I stood my ground and argued that I didn't want to go home, I wanted to stay in school. Finally, it was agreed that I could stay as long as I did not leave the Principals office and stayed away from the windows.

Later that day I rode with my parents to go over my Grandmother's house on the west side of town. As we crested over the bridge on Branner Street I finally saw why my Principal had been so fearful. The grocery store on the corner of Fourth and Branner was gone. All that remained were smoldering blackened remains. The store was only a few years old and the only grocery store close to that neighborhood. We had shopped there many times. Now it laid in ruin, and to this day, it has never been rebuilt. It was on that day that I began to wake up to the world that my parents had tried so hard to shield us from.

Our parents finally realized that an open conversation was needed. So they sat us down and explained as simply as they could what was going on. It wasn't that we had never seen discrimination before. I remember that a few years prior we had traveled to Memphis, AR to visit our dad's brother Uncle Ray and his family. We had stopped to get gas and the attendant informed us that he couldn't service our car because we were black. My dad calmly explained to the attendant that we were on empty, but still he would not give us gas. I remember that we barely made it back to the "Black" gas station on the other side of town. But what our parents were disclosing to us now was a lot to process. It was frightening that we could be hated or killed just because of the color of our skin. The reality of the world had finally revealed itself to me, and now I knew that I could never close my eyes in hopes that it would all go away.

There was so much that we did not know and understand about being Black in this country. We had been conditioned to ignore and not to acknowledge the injustice that was plaguing our community. But suddenly the world had intruded behind the curtain that our parents had constructed in our lives and the ugliness of racism had demanded to be seen and heard. When entering the highly integrated Topeka High School, I remember feeling very intimidated. Of course, we eventually overcame this dilemma. But it became evident that something different had to be done with our younger sisters. We did not want them to have to go through the cultural blight that we had endured.

The sisters who were next in line where Pam and Cheryl. Behind them came Yvonne and our infant sister Tiffany and five years later our sister Talisha. We had a legacy of sisters to protect and educate about our culture.

A few years had passed since our awakening, and now the time had come for Pam to enter our neighborhood Jr. High School (Holiday Junior High). So, we went to Momma and Daddy and begged them not to send her to the still racially unbalanced school. They declined our request until two years later when Cheryl was promoted to Junior High. We went before our parents again with our plea and Surprisingly, our parents listened and decided that it might be best to send Pam and Cheryl to a school over by our grandmother called Boswell Jr. High. Boswell Jr. High was much different from Holiday Jr. High. Its student population was considerably more balanced. Our cousin Debbie had attended there, and she liked it, so Momma and Daddy decided to give it a try.

As the school year began, everything seemed to be going very well for Pam and Cheryl. They quickly made new friends and adjusted admirably to the social changes within the school. They also were enjoying the notoriety of being the "new girls" on the block. Their fame entitled them to many exclusive perks at the new school, which is why we believe they became so emboldened. We watched our sisters with pride, as they progressed at first in their new environment, but what we did not see were the hidden pitfalls that came along with that change.

The first clue that things were going wrong was that Pam and Cheryl's grades began to drop drastically. Momma and Daddy also began receiving phone calls from their teachers, stating that their attitudes were bridging on disrespect. Then one day, the ultimate folly happened! Cheryl, the one who was always the quiet, sensitive one of the siblings, was accused by her teacher of throwing paper on the floor. The teacher asked her to pick it up. But Cheryl, with her newfound weapon (her mouth), declared that she was not the one who threw it down, and then loudly announced that she was not going to pick it up!

Well, direct defiance of a teacher was punishable by a few days' suspension, and Cheryl was tried and convicted by the principal of this offense. Before long, Momma arrived at the school to escort Cheryl home. Before this incident, none of us, except Wayne, had ever been in this type of trouble. You could almost expect this from Wayne because boys were always fighting, but not from our little sister Cheryl; and never for disrespecting a teacher.

Daddy frequently worked two jobs, one in the morning and one in the evening. Unfortunately for Cheryl, Daddy happened to be off on her "kick-out" day. As Momma and Cheryl entered the house, Cheryl slowly eased herself through the front door, with her large wide eyes filled to the brim with tears. Momma must have informed her already that Daddy was home. Momma pointed her to the doorway leading into the Dining Room, as we heard Daddy's voice booming through the house, "Cheryl, come here!" We all knew what would happen next. We had renamed the Dining Room "The Whipping Room" many years prior.

As Cheryl entered the Dining Room, Daddy was standing there waiting on her. We heard him ask her why she had been disobedient at school and got kicked out. Cheryl gave the same patent answer that we always gave, which was "I don't know." He began scolding her about being disrespectful, then followed up his words with a spanking.

Momma stood there, listening and I could see the disappointment in her eyes. We had sold her on the move of schools, and she really wanted it to work. We all knew that Pam and Cheryl's days of Exodus had now ended. All that we had worked for was now gone literally by the drop of a paper.

The next day Pam and Cheryl were enrolled back at our neighborhood school. Soon their grades rebounded, and their personalities returned to normal. We all learned the meaning of the old saying "The grass always appears greener on the other side." We thought that our sisters needed more cultural exposure and had even convinced our parents of that need. But what we learned was that change takes time. We had adjusted. And we knew with their short time exposure, that our sister would adapt also.

Lessons Learned: Change never occurs without conflict.

> *There is a time for everything, and a season*
> *for every activity under the heavens*
> *Ecclesiastes 3:1*

The Giants Reign

Baby Sister Tiffany, Carol and Niece Mckeeba

"Fe, Fi, Foe, Fum, I smell the blood of an English man's."

These words were remarkably familiar to me during my childhood. They represented years of watching and reading the "Jack and the Beanstalk" story. The story never really scared me. Instead, it mostly annoyed me that Jack would foolishly exchange the family cow for a hand full of beans when his family needed food. After being discarded, the magic beans grew into a gigantic beanstalk reaching up to the "Land of the Giants." Jack then invaded the privacy of a giant who was living his life and minding his own business. Jack next sought to steal the Giant's precious possession, which was the goose that laid the golden eggs so that he and his family on earth could become rich.

I did sympathize with the invasion that the Giant endured, but the presence of the Giants' size and booming voice was frightening. I would cringe whenever I heard the "Fe Fi Fo Fum" taunting that the Giant echoed before capturing his victims. Somehow, his words became a permanent part of my childhood, in the form of a re-occurring nightmare.

For many years I would dream that I was playing outside with my friends and siblings when I would hear a loud wailing sound. Instinctively all the characters in the dream would scream, "The Giant is coming!" Everyone would then scatter to find a hiding place, with mine always being my parent's closet. Invariably the Giant seemed to always know where I was hiding. He would predictably rip off my house's roof, reach into the closet, and pull me from my hiding place kicking and screaming. He then would ceremonially eat me limb by limb. I continued to have this dream at least once-a-month, with the outcome always being the same.

As I grew into my pre-teen years, I hoped that the nightmare would end, but they didn't! They didn't come as often, but they still came. One day my older sister Belinda and I were talking about our dreams, and she told me that I could control my dreams by merely making an escape plan before I went to sleep. So, I began to devise several strategies that could change the nightmare's outcome and render me victorious.

However, no matter how creative or inventive the hiding places became, the Giant would find me, pluck me out, then gobble me up. I remember dreaming up hiding places inside the house walls, but the Giant would still sniff me out, call out his Fe, Fi, Foe, Fum, dismantle the house, pull me out, and eat me. Regrettably, my plans for controlling my dreams seemed to fail every time.

The dream became very frustrating, and as I grew into a teenager, and was still having the nightmare, I gave in to the fact that it would always be a part of my life. Then one day, when I was about sixteen years old, while I was outside playing with my baby sister Tiffany, I heard the same loud wailing sound from my dream. Instantly my subconscious mind yelled out to my conscious mind – "The Giant is coming!"

I instinctively tried to think quickly of a place to hide! But just as suddenly, I realized that I did not hear the giants menacing words filling the air. At this point, I laughingly reminded myself that I was not in a dream! I began to evaluate my feelings at that point, which solved why the nightmare had mysteriously haunted me for so long.

Our family home was approximately two blocks away from the Santa Fe Railroad hub. And every day at noon, the shop whistles blew, letting the workers know that it was lunchtime. I finally realized that the sound that summoned the giant in my dream was the sound of the Santa Fe whistles. At some point, during my childhood, I had associated the loud, startling sound of the Santa Fe whistles with my fear of the Giant's uncontrollable size. Since I had suppressed the fear that the sound produced, I continued to have my nightmare. After realizing the connection, I began to laugh. My sister Tiffany didn't understand why I was laughing, but she laughed with me also. From that moment on, I was never haunted again by that nightmare.

Ironically, later in life, when I became a Mom, I would chase my children to their bedrooms to the tune of, "Fe, Fi, Foe, Fum, I smell the blood of an English man." I would follow up with tickles and hugs as they giggled and hid beneath their covers.

The Giant's words had now lost their power. No longer did they trouble my thoughts. The haunting words from my childhood had now been transformed into a game that my children lovingly remember and cherish.

Lesson learned: We only fear those things that we do not understand!

(2ⁿᵈ Timothy 1:7) For God has not given us a spirit of fear, but of power and of love and of a sound mind

After 5

(All Dressed Up and Nowhere to Go)

Carol, Ready for the Daisy Chain

Why didn't I just tell them that plans had changed and that I was no longer going! It would have been just that easy, but instead, I played the day as if nothing were wrong.

I had met this amazing boy. He was so, so handsome. He was a senior at Topeka high school, and I was a sophomore. It wasn't often back then that a sophomore would have the rare opportunity to attend the Junior-Senior Prom.

I was so extremely excited when I told my Mom that I had been invited to the Prom. Her first question was, "Are you sure you are allowed to attend?" "Yes, Momma," I replied. "As long as a Junior or Senior invite you, you can attend." Of course, Momma called the school and checked, and once it was confirmed, she joined my excitement, and the hunt for a dress was on!

We must have shopped every store in Topeka from White lakes Mall to the stores on the Kansas Avenue strip, before landing at the front door of one of the most prestigious stores downtown: Pelletier's. Pelletier's was much different than Sears or JC Penney's. They had a special person whose only job was to open the door when you arrived. The store was beautiful and had gorgeous sales ladies who silently smiled at you as they stood stoically behind their glass counters. The store was quiet and serene. Momma must have known where she was going because she politely nodded at the sales ladies and walked directly to the elevator at the back of the store and pushed the up button. I heard the elevator cables crank into motion, and before long, the doors spanned open, and there stood a man with a gray uniform trimmed in red piping and wearing a cap likened to a coiffure. I couldn't believe that this store had what I would call an "Elevator Man!" He kindly asked us the floor that we would like to go to, then strongly announced the floor number as the doors folded open again.

This must have been the "Special Dress Floor" because in front of us were several racks of the most beautiful dresses that I had ever seen. How was I to choose? Which one would earn the right to accompany me to the coveted dance of the season? Momma began the search, pulling one dress after another from the rack. Some earned the immediate "No" vote while others won a trip to the dressing room, but none of them at that moment had qualified for the trip home. Momma then suggested that we check the clearance rack, and it was there that I would find my friend, my heart, my incredibly special dress!

The dress was made of golden satin with long Victorian shaped sleeves and had a high Victorian collar trimmed with lace. I had always admired the long, beautiful dresses the ladies wore in the old musicals that I liked to watch on the television, and this dress made me feel like one of them. The fabric was soft and flowed beautifully from the empire waistline to the floor while the light danced off its sheen. It was both simple and elegant at the same time. Yes, this would be the dress that would begin my high school memories. But there was only one problem. Even though it was on the clearance rack, it was still above the amount Momma had wanted to spend. But she could see that I had already fallen in love with the dress and decided to purchase it for me anyway.

The clerk rang up the purchase and placed my newfound companion into a fancy clothing bag that bore the name of "Pelletier's" and zipped it up. I proudly carried the bag down the elevator, through the store and out the door to my car; visualizing how I would look as I flowed through the doors of my first Prom.

I spent the next few days at school planning what my boyfriend would wear and when he would pick me up. Everything was going as planned until Friday, the day before the Prom. I'm not sure what happened. I will chalk it up to my immaturity. My boyfriend was walking me to class, and for some reason, I got angry with him. He may have looked at another girl or maybe someone had told someone to tell me that someone saw him talking to someone else! Whatever the reason for our small argument, I heard myself say two words that would haunt me the rest of my sophomore year.

I snatched my books out of his hands and yelled, "We're through!!" He just stood there and looked at me in disbelief. He responded with, "You know that if you break up with me, you can't go to the Prom tomorrow!" I just smiled and said – "Yes, I can." "You already brought the tickets, and my name is on the list! I'll just go by myself!" He laughed at me and said, "It doesn't matter, Carol, if your name is on the list, a junior or senior has to be with you to get in. It's the rule!" I just looked at him and said, "We'll see!" Then I turned and walked into my class.

I knew in my heart that he was right, but I allowed my pride to get the best of me. I was hoping that he would come after me and say that he was sorry and ask to make up. But instead, he turned and walked away also. It wasn't just the Prom, he was a nice guy, and I knew that the "He Said, She Said" stuff wasn't true. I had tried to play an old boyfriend game and lost. Now I had to go home and tell my mother that the dress I loved and the dress that she had so proudly searched for and sacrificed for would not be going to the Prom.

When I arrived home from school, Momma had a list of

things to get me ready for the following day's Prom. I swallowed hard and then spurted out..."I broke up with my boyfriend today!" I saw this horrifying look cross my mother's face, so I quickly lied and said..."But, my name is on the list, so I should still be able to go." Momma looked somewhat relieved, but asked if I was sure? My mouth kept lying, and I kept hoping that what I was saying would somehow come true. "Yeah, I talked to the office today, and they said it shouldn't be a problem."

Saturday morning started like any prep day for the Prom should. I got my hair done, purchased pantyhose, and even topped it off with a corsage, just in case my date was still angry and didn't get me one. My Mom, all the while, kept asking, "Are you sure you can still go?"

The evening soon arrived, and before I knew it, I was standing in the middle of the living room floor wearing my fabulous golden dress. I felt like a queen. My sisters and brother commented on how pretty I looked and wished me well. Momma and Daddy both decided that they wanted to drive me since my dress was so long. I had planned to drive myself, and then if I wasn't able to get in, I could go to my cousin Lennie's house and hang out with her until it was time to go home. Now they wanted to take me, so I had to come up with a plan B fast!

I strolled out to the car and slid into the back seat of Daddy's car and rode in silence to the school. As I was getting out of the car, I looked back at my parents and said, "I don't know if the lady I talked to at school Friday is at the check-in table. Can you wait just in case I can't get in?" Daddy agreed, but Momma gave me a look that said: "You know you aren't getting in." I knew that she was just hoping that maybe my lie would somehow come true also.

So, I got out of the car and strolled along the long sidewalk up to the school with the other couples that were happily going to the Prom. I let the others check in first, and then, I approached the check-in table. One of the teachers asked, "Carol, where is your date? I looked at her and said, "He's supposed to meet me here." She looked at the list then said, "Well, he has already checked in and said you weren't coming." I looked at them and said, "Well, we broke up, but my name is on the list, isn't it?' She just gave me this sad look, shook her head no, and said, "You can only get in if you're with an upperclassman."

I knew what her answer would be. I wasn't shocked, just embarrassed that I had foolishly believed my fictitious deception. That chapter of my sophomore year ended much differently than I had imagined. No Cinderella ending. I held my head high and tried to hide the tears that were finding their way to the corners of my eyes and made the long walk back to my chariot that was awaiting me by the curb. I returned to the back seat with no questions and fought to keep my tears from falling on my beautiful satin dress. I arrived back home and went straight to my room. I unrobed my Golden Prom dress and placed it gently into its garment bag and slowly zipped it into its resting place. My beautiful dress would hang in my closet for another year, emerging to accompany me as a participant of the "Daisy Chain" at the next year's Graduation. Not exactly its intended purpose.

**Lesson Learned: Don't play games that
you are not prepared to lose.**

Spotty

(The Neighborhood Terror)

No Lesson. Just a Memory.

In just about every neighborhood lives a dog whose sole purpose in life is to terrorize the inhabitants of that neighborhood. In our community, that dog's name was Spotty.

Spotty lived in the pretty pink house at the end of our block. The house had fencing protecting the whole yard except the area by their driveway, and this was the area where Spotty laid in wait, day in and day out. There were not any leash laws back then, so it wasn't unusual to see dogs running free. Spotty was a medium size dog with long wavy black hair and loved to show his mouth full of pearly white teeth.

We had to pass by Spotty's house every morning as we headed out to school, and every morning Spotty would lay in wait to bark at us and chase us for the length of his block. It didn't matter which direction we chose to walk to try to avoid Spotty. If we went through the alley in the back of the house, Spotty would be there. If we went the opposite direction and went around the block, Spotty would somehow know and meet us at the far corner for our daily chase. Spotty controlled all activity at the end of the block.

I remember one day coming home from school and seeing Spotty lying asleep. He had the usual dog sleep position, you know, rolled over on his back with the legs dangling in the air. I thought maybe I could sneak past him and make it home without being chased, but I was wrong. As I approached him and was almost past, he rolled his head toward me and seemed almost to smile as he jumped to his feet and chased me the rest of the way home.

I don't believe that Spotty would have ever gotten any exercise if we had not moved into the neighborhood. I don't even think that he would have bitten us if he were to catch us. I believe that he just liked to see us run. It was just that simple; he sensed our fear and used it as a form of daily play. This scenario continued throughout our grade school years and into junior high. In a sick kind of way, we sort of looked forward to Spotty's daily chase.

As he grew older, he wasn't able to chase us as much. The last time that I saw Spotty was after I had graduated from High School. His chase had been consumed by arthritis, but his bark remained true. It was almost sad to see him aging because that also meant that I too was getting older.

I've heard it said that everything changes to remain the same. I believe this statement is true because dogs will still chase, and people will always run; it is just the players of the game that change. As for Spotty, he will forever hold a place in our memories.

The Warning

Carol 18yrs old

As we enter our independent teenage years, we tend to forget those small but essential lessons we may have learned as a child. I guess we believe that the rules no longer apply and that now we are old enough and wise enough to make our own decisions. These years mark the time of ultimate growth and expansion as individuals. We are encouraged to make our own decisions and to express our thoughts openly, but there are times, believe it or not, when our parents still know what is best.

I was eighteen, out of high school, and just beginning my first year at Washburn University. Like many other girls my age, my main course of study was boys! On this evening, my best friends, Renee' and Gail, and I wanted to ride out to the Holiday Inn on the south side of town. We had heard from reliable sources that a college track team was in town and that the hotel would be packed with lots of fine, young men. We decided that we would go and investigate the stock after Renee' got off work.

Mom and Dad had decided to go to Leavenworth that evening to visit Momma's sister, who we called Aunt Singie. We never knew why everyone called her Singie because her real name was Barbara. In the past, you could not have kept us away from Aunt Singie's house. In fact, we use to cry when we had to leave her home. But since we were now "grown," we chose to pursue a different type of entertainment. My younger sisters still went on the trip with Mom and Dad, but my brother Wayne and I had the privileged of pursuing teenage activities with our friends.

As my parents were preparing to leave, my mom abruptly turned to us and said, "I want the two of you to stay at home while we're gone." Wayne didn't have anywhere to go that night, so he said, "That's cool with me." I, on the other hand, had plans, so I protested loudly. Momma again demanded that I stay at home. Her command was somewhat unusual since we were old enough to be out without our parent's permission. The only thing we had to be sure of was that we were in at a decent hour. So what made this day so different puzzled me.

Momma and Grandma were what you could call "Dreamers." They would have a dream about something or someone, and then the dream would inevitably come true. It was kind of spooky, but Momma thought of it as a blessing. I had always joked with them about their dreams and would tell them not to dream about me. So, Momma was a little hesitant about reveling to me why I could not go out. Finally, she just said, "I have a bad feeling about you being out tonight." It never occurred to me that she had received a warning concerning my fate that evening, I thought she just wanted us to stay home because they were going to be out of town. But I had my own plans. So I falsely agreed to stay home and waited for them to leave.

As they pulled out of the driveway, I jumped on the phone and called my friend Gail. She was just as excited as I was about the evening events and was ready to get things moving. We discussed who would drive that night and where we would meet. My other friend Renee' was working her job at McDonald's that evening, so we decided that it would be best if we met at her job. We had two cars to choose to cruise in that night. Gail's cool green Ford Mustang, or "Brownie," my tan colored 1966 Plymouth Valiant. I remember when I first got Brownie. I was so disappointed when my father brought it home because I wanted a small sporty car, not a medium-sized box. But once I got behind Brownies wheel, we had become fast friends. But, Brownie was low on gas that night, so we agreed to ride in Gail's car, and to leave mine at McDonald's.

We knew when we arrived at the hotel that the evening wasn't going to be as we had planned. The marquee displayed words of welcome to the visiting track team, but there wasn't a guy in sight. It was after 10 pm now, and the hotel's lobby was locked. We figured that the track team had probably gone to bed early to get ready for their meet. We decided to ride around the parking lot anyway, to see who we could see, but it was to no avail. Soon we got bored and since there was nothing else to do, we agreed that it was time to go home. I knew that my parents generally returned from Leavenworth around midnight, so I still had plenty of time to return home before they arrived.

We dropped Renee' home first, then Gail dropped me back at McDonald's to pick up my car. I jumped into my car, waved goodbye and headed home. I was happy that I didn't have far to go; just over the railroad tracks and a couple of bridges, and I would be at my destination. I was about a mile from home when Brownie began to stutter and jerk. Brownie had always been an exceptionally reliable car, so I became concerned when it started to malfunction. As I began crossing the railroad tracks, Brownie started to jerk more violently. I thought to myself, "What's going on?" Brownie then came to a complete stop straddled across a set of railroad tracks (and you guessed it) the train signals began to flash! My first thought was to jump out of the car and run to the bridge in front of me, but I couldn't abandon Brownie on the tracks.

I immediately started pumping the gas pedal while begging Brownie to start. I remembered seeing a similar scene in a movie on TV, and I had yelled at the people to get out of the car! Even though I knew that I should get out of the car and run to safety, I just kept on franticly pumping the gas. I could see the bright circular headlight of the train quickly approaching and could hear its long deep horn getting closer and closer, warning me to get off the tracks. By this time, I was screaming at Brownie to "Go, Go." I again looked out my window only to see the train bounding swiftly upon me. When the train had reached within fifty feet of me, Brownie roared to life, lunged forward, climbed the small bridge past the tracks, and sputtered to silence again as it reached the top.

I sat there, trembling with the thought of what had almost happened. I started telling myself to calm down so that I could figure out what was wrong with the car. I reasoned that my lights were still on, so it couldn't be the battery. The engine continued to make a whining sound as I turned the key, so it appeared that it wasn't the starter. There was only one explanation left. I was out of gas. I turned on the interior light and looked at the gas meter and saw that it was registering "Empty!"

About this time a big white conversion van with a man and a woman inside, crested the bridge top traveling in the opposite direction. The train was still occupying the tracks, so they stopped, and the man got out. He walked over to my car and yelled through the window, "do you need help?" Mom and

Dad had trained us never to roll the window down if we were stranded and to refuse help from strangers. They instructed us to go to a nearby phone booth to call home and if that wasn't available, to put on our trouble lights, and wait for a police officer. My trouble lights were on, my door was locked, and my window was up. But here I was at eleven o'clock at night with no phone booth or Police Officer in sight. I reasoned that the man did have his wife or girlfriend with him, so it should be okay to let him help.

I rolled my window down about a few inches and told the man that I believe I was out of gas. He asked me to turn the key to make sure, but the car still would not start. He then replied in a sympathetic voice, "Awwww, that's too bad." I quickly turned my head and looked at him through the slightly lowered window. Something had changed about his voice. It now had a ring of sinister cruelty and I recognized immediately that I was in danger. So I quickly grabbed the crank to close the gap in the window and was extremely relieved to see that I had not unlocked the door.

I immediately began to roll the window up, but just as quickly the man stuck his hands in the window opening and began to push down. He kept saying, "I've never dated a black girl before." A chill rippled down my spine, and I began to feel as though I was in an awful nightmare. I also realized that none of this would be happening if I had only followed Momma's directions to stay home. It was too late for regrets, I was in trouble, and there was no one around to help me.

I continued struggling with the window while also reaching for the only weapon I possessed, a butter knife in my glove box. I don't remember why I had it in there; I just remember finding it under my seat when I cleaned my car earlier that week. The man continued speaking to me while trying to reach me through the small opening in the window. I no longer was listening to what he was saying but did notice that the tone of his voice was becoming even colder and more demanding. I continued to keep pressure on the window crank while trying my best to retrieve the knife from the glove box. I could still hear the train moving swiftly on the tracks behind me and began to pray that the Lord would send help.

Suddenly, I heard a group of new voices yelling, "Hey, What Are You Doing!"

The man and I both looked up at the same time and saw a group of about six or seven young black men jumping out of an old cargo van, running towards us. The man then jerked his hands out of the window, ran back to his van, and sped across the now vacant railroad tracks. I must have still been screaming when they reached me because I kept hearing them say, "Carol, it's alright, open the door!" I finally focused in on their faces and realized that they were friends of mine from school. I thought to myself, "God has heard my prayer." I continued crying as I unlocked the door and tried to tell them about running out of gas and how "the Man" had tried to get me out of the car. They became furious and asked if I would like them to chase the van down. I immediately answered, no! The only thing I wanted to do was to go to my home. So, they helped me out of my car, into their van, and drove me to my house. (The next day I found out that they had searched the whole city trying to find that white van.)

My brother Wayne had a puzzled look on his face as I entered our house flanked on all sides by my rescuers. They helped explain, as best they could, what had happened as I headed for the large plush chair in the corner of the room. I don't believe that I ever realized how safe home felt. They offered to take us back to get my car, but Wayne declined and said that he would drive me to pick-up my car. I relaxed and let my head roll back into the chair, while my brother went out to the shed to get the gas can. Luckily, there was still gas in it from when Daddy had cut the grass earlier that day.

On the drive back to my car, I told Wayne the full story

of the night's events. As we crested the curve of the bridge, there sat Brownie, gleaming under the clear starlit sky. Brownie looked so peaceful with the moonlight dancing off his hood. I thought to myself, "How could this have been the scene of an almost tragic night." Wayne parked his car opposite mine and began to feed the gas into Brownie's empty tank. The streets were entirely vacant now, except for a set of headlights moving quickly across the railroad tracks. My heart started racing as the oncoming car began to slow. I thought to myself, "Oh no, not again!" Wayne must have noticed the dread in my eyes and instinctively stepped forward to protect me from any further danger.

When the nearing vehicle pulled to a stop, we were relieved to see Momma and Daddy peering through the window of our family car. They didn't yell at me or drill me with questions. They just quickly got out of their car to assist us. Daddy inquired about what had happened, and I, like a guilt-ridden convict, confessed to all the night's events. Momma just listened, then said, "I told you to stay home." (I found out later that Momma had a feeling that I was in trouble and had instructed Daddy to take a different exit when coming home from Leavenworth. That exit would bring them directly to where I was.)

The night ended with no further incident. I had learned a

lesson that some would never get an opportunity to tell. My disobedience could have led to my demise; instead, my life had been spared twice that night. As Brownie and I traveled home with my brother and parents in tow, I *whispered, "Thank You, God."*

Lesson Learned: You never get too old for good advice.

Children, obey your parents in the Lord, for this is right. "Honor your father and mother"...which is the first commandment with a promise..."so that it may go well with you and that you may enjoy long life on the earth." Ephesians 6:1-3

Always and Forever

Theodus and Carol – June 1978

Everyone loves a great love story. A heartwarming girl meets boy, love-at-first sight, sweep you off your feet, love-story. Some believe that this kind of love is only for Hollywood or fairytales. I read once that love is destined and that many couples have already crossed paths with their "Spouse to be" years before they actually notice each other, and that fate, somehow, destines them to meet at just the right time.

I have always been a dreamer with one foot in this world and the other finding its way in fantasy. I believed in the magic of goodness; if you were kind to others, others would be nice to you, and that life would always find a way to reward you with your heart's desires.

Even as a little girl, I loved a good love story. I enjoyed reading all the fairy tales like Cinderella and Sleeping Beauty, and heavily fantasized about who my Prince Charming would be. I fancied the scenario of the girl who loved the guy, and he loved her, but he didn't realize that he did. She would turn away saddened that he did not feel the same way about her. But before the movie was over, he would find her and rescue her from her brokenness, gathering her in his arms, and declaring to her his undying love. Then they would ride off into the sunset, happily ever after! That was the pattern of every love story that I have witnessed. I found myself addicted to happy endings. And I believed that somehow, my life would play out the same way.

When I think about it, I believe that my desire to be romantically loved outweighed all my life goals. I was a high achiever in school and had dreams of vocational directions. But my most prominent goal was to find my true love. There were a few good prospects along the journey, but unfortunately, the relationships mostly ended with no promise of a "Happy Ever After." When I think back, I could partly be to blame in my relationship failures. I always kept my deep feelings hidden and seldom shared them. I figured if a guy wanted to know me that he would take time to work past my barriers to earn my inner thoughts. But what I discovered later in life, is that it is the honest revealing of yourself to the right person that gives you emotional strength. I hated playing love games. Why couldn't we just exchange notes that said, "Mark here if you love me." If the answer was no, then you could just move on.

I remember that one New Year's Eve, my best friend Renee' and I formed a "Spinsters Anonymous Club" because both she and I had ended up alone on the most important night of the year. Later that year Renee' even made membership cards to the club. The cards brought levity to our situations, and instead of being sad, we celebrated our friendship instead. Our membership lasted for a few months, then a new love interest came into each of our lives, and the club dissolved.

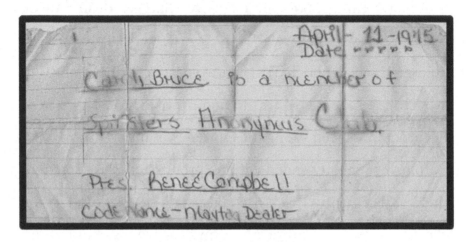

Spinsters Anonymous Membership Card

I remember in the late 1970s, after a very hurtful break-up, that I swore off dating ever again. I prayed to God and said, "I will wait until you send me my husband. Until then, I give up!" I had dated this one man for more than three years before the relationship dissolved. I had convinced myself that he was "The One," but different situations in our courtship kept screaming at me that I was wrong. One day we both just turned and walked away from each other and never looked back. I had invested my heart with the wrong person, and it had crushed me.

I gathered the broken pieces of my emotions and hid them deep beneath my pride and moved forward into my life. I reasoned that the everlasting, "Happy Ever After", love-story does not happen for everyone. I was through with relationships. I laid my dreams under my pillow and left it all in God's hands. If I were to be happy, God would have to provide it. I was no longer going to trust myself to choose.

I gave up the party scene and going out every weekend night. I started changing my life and the choices that I had been making. I shifted my attention to family and friends only. I was approached many times with offers for a date, but I had refused them. I just knew that they were not the ones. Then without notice, it happened while I was at work.

I had been employed at Sears Department Store as an associate in the Credit Department for more than a year. The department in which I worked, was located on the 2nd floor of the store. My position was to handle and maintain credit card accounts. My job also included answering phones and helping the walk-in customers that came to the front counter. It would be there, behind that counter, that I would be gifted with my "Forever After."

It was early afternoon and I was standing back by the bank of phones talking to my coworker Rosemary. We were making sure to keep eyes on the counter as we waited for possible customers to approach. We watched as a group of people were exiting the escalator located in the middle of the sales floor in front of us. That is when it happened. I saw this tall, handsome man as he stepped off the escalator and turned towards our area. I felt my breath stop, and then I heard myself say, "Oh my God! There's my husband!"

Rosemary turned and looked at me with a puzzled look and asked, "What did you say?" I was stunned that I had blurted those words out loud. I had no idea where they came from, especially since I wasn't even thinking about a relationship. I gave a nervous laugh and said, "I think I said there's my husband?" I thought to myself that maybe this was the answer to my prayers. The one that God had hand-picked and sent to me. Could it be this easy?

I approached the counter, making sure I stayed professional. Plus, I had to check this guy out to see if he was the one. He gave me his name (Theodus) and then began inquiring about his credit account. I answered his questions quickly, but then he inquired, "How can I find out about the insurance coverage I have on my children?" I have never been one to hide my emotions, so when I heard "children," I immediately assumed that he was married. The emotion of that thought must have registered in my eyes because he quickly corrected and said, "No, no...I mean, I'm divorced. They live with my ex-wife." My eyes lit up again, and I smiled (I am sure even brighter) and told him that I would have to research his question. As the conversation ended, he asked me to call him once I had gathered the information. I agreed, but then later that day I decided to just mail a formal letter with my findings instead. I wasn't in the habit of calling guys. And I knew that his invitation to call was less than professional. I figured that if he were interested that he would get back in touch with me.

A couple of weeks had passed, and I had not heard back from Theodus, so I assumed that maybe my intuition was wrong. I had all but forgotten about him until while working one afternoon I heard a familiar voice ask, "Can I speak to Carol?" I turned around, and there he stood again. The very one that I had written off as a mistake. He began with, "I thought you were going to call me." And I answered, "Didn't you get the company letter?" The conversation went back and forth and then ended with smiles, laughter, and an invitation to accompany him to the Denver Bronco vs Chiefs football game that weekend. Like the many love stories, I had viewed so often on the TV screen, our courtship went up, down, and around for several months. There were misunderstandings, break-ups, and then a New Year's Eve make-up. Then a few months later, one warm spring afternoon, he asked the question that I had dreamt of hearing my whole adult life.

I had come to visit Theodus at his home, and he kept nervously pacing back and forth in the room. I was sitting on the couch making small talk, not sure what was going on. I thought that maybe he wanted to end our relationship. He finally stopped pacing, put his hands on his hips, cleared his throat, and then asked, "Sooo...Do you want to get married?" I was shocked! They were not the exact words I had imagined that my husband-to-be would voice. I was hoping for a proclamation of some type like, "Carol, you are the love of my life, and I can't imagine living another day without you. I love you. Will you marry me?" My next thought was, "Shouldn't he be down on one knee?"

I had rehearsed this scene all my life. But as the moment unfolded, it wasn't anything like I had imagined. I was caught entirely off guard. I knew that I loved him, but I wasn't sure if I could trust myself to judge my feelings. Then I remembered how God had spoken to me that day at work and had told me, "There's your husband!" So, I accepted the "Standing up, pacing back and forth, hand on his hips; "Sooo, do you want to get married," proposal, and I replied with a just as simple, "Sure!"

I was convinced that this should be the moment when music

should fill the air and doves would scatter happily into the heavens. But I quickly found out that real life is not a movie and many times scenes will not play out as perfectly as we orchestrate them in our minds. My fantasy had become a reality. Not exactly how I imagined. But it had happened!

Well, here we are 42 years later. Still together! It wasn't easy. We had many happy, exciting times and some not so pleasant, unbelievably bad times. There were a few obstacles that I did not think we would make it past. But the "Ever After" proved to be more resilient than the adversity. But, when I examined the vows that we took on that romantic wedding day, I discovered that the vows were preparing us for the reality of the days to come.

> *"I take thee, to have and to hold from this day forward, for better, for worse, for richer, for poorer, in sickness and in health, to love and to cherish, till death do us part."*

These vows do not pretend to promise a "Happy Ever After." They detail a pledge to each other to hang in there, even though the "Happy" is not present. It stipulates a commitment that the two of you will hold tight to the "After" as you find your way out the other side of your difficulty.

I discovered that "Happily Ever After" never rides off into the sunset. It actually hangs around, waiting to be invited into your union. I also found that it is very needy and demands to be pampered and fed continuously. It proved harder to maintain than raising our children. A child will give and accept your love with no strings attached. But I quickly learned that "Happy Ever After" requires so much more to solidify its place in your Love Story. This type of love craves nurturing, work, and compromise every step of the way. I have learned over the years that every breakthrough and every victory anchor the "Happy Ever After" more securely in your relationship.

I questioned many times while in the midst of an argument or disagreement, if my husband truly were the correct one that God had sent me? I would joke that maybe there was a cute short guy behind him that I failed to notice. But all kidding aside, I knew without question that this was the man that God had sent to me. I knew because God had spoken to me through my own words. God used our relationship with all its ups and downs to wake me up. He wanted to force me out of my fantasy world and to allow the real Carol to live. My husband and I became each other's scrubbing boards, and as our rough edges began to fall, the "Ever After" settled to take its place within our marriage.

So, What about the subject of fate? The theory that destiny forces us together and that our paths have already crossed before we meet.

As Theodus and I got to know more about each other, we discovered that our paths had crossed at least twice before our meeting. When I introduced him to my best friend Renee', she looked at me and said, "Carol, I already know him! You and I use to pass by him at Washburn several times a week. He would be coming out the north door of the student union while we were going in." That was crazy because, until that day at Sears, I had never noticed him.

The other cross meeting was when I was a little girl around 10yrs old.

When my husband came to meet my parents, he noted that they lived across the street from his good friend Bunny Harris. Bunny and his Sisters were our childhood babysitters. He mentioned that when he was eighteen while visiting Bunny, he returned to his car, and one of the tires was flat. He said he looked across the street and saw my sister Belinda, brother Wayne and myself sitting on the curb laughing and pointing at the tire. He thought that we had flattened his tire, and of course, we hadn't. But at our age, everything was funny. After telling the story, he looked at me and said, "Hey, you were the little girl sitting on the curb!" I still tease Theodus even today about that first meeting, saying, "Just think; You married the little girl sitting on the curb." Fate, Wow!

I would love to take a glimpse of God's storyboard of my life. I wonder how many times God looked at my choices and just shook his head with a little smirk on his face (just like my father used to do) happy that I finally got it right.

Lessons Learned: Life happens when
you let go and let life happen.

Jeremiah 29:11 For I know the plans I have for you,"
declares the LORD, "plans to prosper you and not
to harm you, plans to give you hope and a future.

A Long Wave Goodbye

Momma, Mckeeba and Carol

I sat up in my bed startled and unsure if I were fully awake. I was seven months pregnant and could feel the baby moving restlessly in my belly. I tried my best to relax in hopes that she would settle down. I then felt the warm streams of fresh tears flowing freely down my face. "Why am I crying?" A deep sadness had settled in my chest, and it felt as if my heart had been broken in two. Little by little, the dream began to mend itself back together in my conscious memory.

I recalled in the dream that my family was leaving my Grandmother Reece's house. Everyone had run down the steps to get in Momma's car, but I was still standing on the porch. Suddenly, a brilliant light filled the sky and radiated down on the porch, engulfing me in its intense rays. I felt so safe and could sense someone speaking to me. I did not recognize the sound of actual words, but I could feel them. They were loud and clear, but silent at the same time. It was as if the light was having a conversation within my soul. My soul then quickly translated the words to my conscious mind. "A Loved One Will Be Taken!" The words were so powerful that they jolted me out of my sleep. "It was just a dream, wasn't it?" I continued to wipe the tears from my eyes. I had never responded to a dream in this manner before. Typically, when I had a nightmare, the memory would quickly fade as I awoke. But this time, the sadness did not go away. I felt it settle and affix itself somewhere deep in my heart. Somehow, I knew what the message meant. I was about to lose either my Mom or Dad!

My husband, Theodus, woke up to find me sitting on the edge of the bed, crying. I couldn't exactly tell him what was wrong. All I could say was that I had a nightmare that felt real. I didn't dare utter the truth of the dream. Plus, how did I know that the message was factual? It could have just been a horrible ugly nightmare. I made a decision not to tell anyone the truth of my vision, because I did not want to give the dream any power to become real! Still, I was not able to sleep for the rest of the night and was relieved to see the sun rising to mark the beginning of a brand-new day. I hoped with all my heart that this new day would somehow cancel the odd night that was finally behind me.

My husband left for work while I made a be-line to my parents' house. I needed to make sure that they were alright, especially since the fragrance of the dream was still so dreadfully strong. I decided that I would be sure to tie up any loose ends or promises that I had made previously with my parents just-in-case the message from the dream was valid.

I believe that my both my Mom and Dad instantly detected that something was amiss. I have never been a person that could hide my emotions very well. The moment I entered their house, I began asking if I could help them with anything? My Dad kind of laughed and said, "Well, I have about five pairs of new pants I still need hemmed." I usually would take two pairs at the most to work on, but this time I said, "Okay" and took the whole stack! My Dad looked at me and said, "Whoa! What's going on?" I covered quickly and replied, "I'm off this weekend and thought this would be a good time to get them done." My Dad gave me a long-puzzled look, then just nodded his head. I took the pants to my car, then returned and joined Momma on the couch to watch her favorite game show, "The Price is Right."

Everything appeared normal with both parents, and for a moment the fear and uncertainty of the dream had disappeared. I told myself, "See, it was just a dream." But as soon as I let my guard down, Momma got quiet. One moment we were calling out prices for the items on the game show, then the next all I heard was my own voice. I turned and looked at Momma, and she was looking at me. Then she said, "I have to talk with you." I asked why she was looking so serious? Then she repeated, "I need to tell you something." Again, I felt the fear from the previous night began to beat simultaneously with the quickening of my own heart.

Momma continued with, "I just need you to listen." She

went on to say, "I had a dream last night..." I thought to myself, "Oh no; Not you too!" She went on to say, "In the dream, there was a funeral. Everyone was here at the house, all our relatives from Kansas and Arkansas. There was a casket, and everyone walked up, one at a time, to look in. I saw all our family there except your sister Belinda. Everyone was searching, trying to find her. When it came my time to look in the casket, I looked in, but the body didn't have a face!" Her eyes began to fill with tears, then she said, "Carol, someone in our family is getting ready to die." As I was looking at her, I saw the same struggle in her eyes that I felt deep in my chest. I had dreamt of a foreboding warning, and I knew that Momma's dream was confirmation.

It had happened too often in the past. Grandma would have a dream, tell it to Momma, then Momma would confirm that she also had a supporting dream. Then, the vision would become a reality. Now, I had become part of the "Circle of Dreamers." Momma looked at me, then asked, "Are you alright?" Did you have a dream also? How did she know??? She must have picked up on my demeanor when I arrived that day. I tried to say, "Yes," but my mind kept screaming, "Don't say anything, then it won't come true." My lips followed my mind as I lied and said, "No. Why?" Momma just looked at me with those mother eyes, searching deep behind my eyes, attempting to see the truth. I know she saw it, but she did not want to know, anymore then I wanted to tell. So, I pretended that all was well.

I finished Daddy's pants and returned them to him the next day. His response was, "Wow! That was fast. Why are you finishing things so quickly"? I looked into his eyes and knew - that he knew - that I knew - that life for our family was about to change. Momma must have told him her dream and that I had the confirmation but would not tell her.

The weekend went as usual. It was the first week of December, which meant "Christmas Shop till You Drop" time. My sisters and I met over at our Parent's house to ride with Momma. Momma was locking up the house when suddenly, she started coughing to the point that she began to choke. Once the coughing was over, she laughed and said, "I hate it when I catch a cold." I had some samples of a new Blue Halls' cough drop that had just come in the mail, so I offered them to her, and they seemed to do the trick. So, we were off to our shopping trip with our first stop being K-mart.

Since it was early afternoon, we decided to eat at the K-mart cafeteria before shopping. I was craving a deep-fried burrito that only K-mart knew how to make. Unfortunately, the cook did a poor job of frying, and the burrito came to me full of grease. Momma snatched the plate from my hand and said, "You are pregnant! You are not going to eat this greasy burrito!!" I was so hungry that I insisted on just eating the parts that were okay. She then glared at me and said, "Carol, you need to stop being so nice and learn to stand up for yourself. You need to start making good decisions for both you and your baby! I won't always be here to help you do that!" Her eyes were so intense, and once again, the sadness that I hoped was just a dream started to throb deep within my core.

Could it be Momma? She was too young. She was only 44 years old. She had much more life to live. She recently had given birth a year ago to my youngest sister Talisha, and five years ago to my sister Tiffany. I shook the thought out of my head and then canceled her from my list of who it could be. I did followed Momma's direction and traded for a perfectly cooked burrito. Then we were off to chase the "Blue light Specials" around the store.

Our last shopping stop of the day was an incredible store called "The Christmas Store." There we found all kinds of cool gifts for different people on our list. I was relieved to see that the day had ended with the family intact, but unfortunately, somewhere along our shopping path my keys had been lost. We figured out by process of elimination that I must have dropped them at The Christmas Store, but the store was closed on Sunday. So Momma agreed to call them first thing Monday morning while I was at work.

Momma called me at work as promised, with the good news that she had found my keys and we made plans for her to bring them to my house after work. I had assured myself that all was well with my family since we had made it through the weekend without incident. Momma arrived at my house at about 5 pm with my keys in tow. We talked and laughed about this and that until it was time for her to go. As she was leaving, she said goodbye to my husband Theodus, but he was so engrossed in whatever was on T.V. that he did not respond. He and Momma always had a secret little battle between them concerning their relationship with me. So, Momma gave a soft laugh, smiled then declared, "Okay, this will be the last time I will say goodbye." Her words shook me and I remember turning quickly to look at her. But she didn't flinch. She just smiled and gave me a one-armed hug.

Momma then headed toward the door and I followed behind her. We said our usual goodbyes while I still inwardly puzzled over what she had just said to my husband. When she got to her car, she turned and smiled again and this time gave what seemed like a long, slow wave goodbye. I stood transfixed, waving back.

I wasn't sure, but I thought I saw a heavy shadowy haze around her? I blinked my eyes to clear my vision and looked again but the haze was still there. Everywhere I looked was clear except for the space around my mother. Immediately, the sadness re-announced itself; only this time, it took residence in my Heart, Spirit, and Soul. There was no question as to why. As Momma drove away, I knew with certainty that it was her! She would be the one to die. I fought my thoughts and cursed myself for allowing my mind to entertain such horrible, morbid thoughts. I fought the truth with prayers and pleading. I fought with all my might. Begging God to not take my Mother. But still, the sadness remained.

That evening I tossed and turned all night, fearing the expectation of the unexpected. Then around midnight the phone rang. My breathing stopped, and all sound fell away around me except for the echo of my husband's voice saying, "Oh no...Oh, no." He hung up the phone and began to cry. My mind was exploding with emotions, and my body was shaking all over. I mustered a shaky, "What Happened?" He went on to say that it was about a family at our church. Their house had caught fire, and their young son had not escaped. We held each other and cried, but at the same time, I felt profound relief that the call was not about my family. More importantly, it was not my Mom! Maybe God had heard my prayers and had chosen someone else to perish? But why this little boy? I felt guilty that I felt relieved that the call wasn't about my Mother. Was it okay that someone else should lose a loved one and not me? I even reasoned that I could have interpreted the warning wrong. Maybe the dream was not about my family after all.

By morning, the feeling of doom was barely detectable, but had been replaced by the compassion that I felt for the family who had just lost their young child. I reported to work still saddened by the previous night's news, but hopeful that all was well for my family. But, around noon I felt the doom stir and then awaken, and then began to claw its way to the forefront of my spirit. I immediately started to get an overwhelming feeling that I needed to call my Mom. For the next few hours, I would find myself picking up the phone receiver to call home and then hanging it up before dialing. My co-worker, Rosemary, noticed my actions then finally asked what I was doing? I was as honest as I could be without sounding "strange." I told her that I feel that I need to call my Mom, but I am afraid that something terrible will happen if I do. I went on to say that I'm hoping that if I didn't call, that everything will be okay. Rosemary just looked at me with a quizzical look then said that she hopes everything works out.

I tried as best as I could to treat the day like any other day. I even suggested to Theo that we go out to eat that evening. I had to develop a plan to drown the growing feeling of calamity inside me, but the fear was relentless and refused to let me go. All I knew was that I had to get as far away from the telephone as possible. Right as we started to leave for the restaurant, the house phone began to ring. I stopped dead in my tracks, looked at my husband, and forcibly demanded that he not answer the phone. He was startled by my odd request but decided to answer it anyway. Suddenly, the previous night's horror began to play out again; only this time, it was my family!

When he hung up, I simply asked, "Is it, Momma?" He gave me a confused look, questioning how I knew. He then confirmed the expected, unexpected news. "Yvonne is on the phone. She said that she thinks your Mom had a stroke or something. She wants us to hurry over there. They have already called the ambulance." We both hurried to the car, and I prayed that Momma would not die; that I would be able to tell her that I loved her and that everything would be alright. Then I remembered my dream from less than a week ago, and then her vision from the same night of a faceless corpus. Then it hit me. She could not see the face because it was her face!

My husband was speeding through the streets and creeping

through red lights, trying to get to Momma as fast as possible. We were about three minutes away when a sudden calm came over me, and I knew that it was over. I reached and touched my husband's arm, with tears flowing down my face and simply said, "It's too late. She's gone." He still hurried on, and within minutes we arrived at my Parent's home. As we pulled to a stop, my sister Yvonne ran over to tell us that the ambulance had just left with Momma. All my sisters and brother converged at the same time. Everyone was there, except my oldest sister Belinda. Yvonne kept asking if Momma would be okay. I did not have the heart to tell her or any of the others no. Plus, I was hoping that maybe something miraculous would change the outcome. So, we all waited.

Daddy had followed the ambulance to the hospital, and Grandma decided to wait with us at the house. We all gathered in the kitchen and the adjacent bedroom. We talked amongst ourselves about things that didn't matter, trying to pass the time and hoping for good news. Our two youngest sisters (Tiffany, who was five years old and Talisha, one-year-old) were playing in the bedroom and having a good time. Before long, we heard Daddy's car gently pulling into the driveway. Right before he entered the house, Tiffany and Talisha both climbed up on the bed and fell into a deep sleep. All the rest of us looked at each other and wondered why they had done that. It was very odd. When I saw them do this, I secretly knew Daddy was coming with bad news.

The front door opened, and Grandma stood up as Daddy entered. Questions started flying in the air immediately; "Where's Momma? Is Momma okay? When is Momma coming home?" Daddy cleared his throat, then looked at the floor, looked at Grandma, then looked back at us. "I'm sorry, your Momma died. She won't be coming home." I watched in horror as his words fell one-by-one like brittle leaves tumbling from a tree in the Fall. It was as if I could see each word that escaped from my Dads mouth, fall and scramble together on the floor; each fracturing the root of our family, and tilting our home on its foundation.

Screams, sobs, and "No, it's not true!" echoed throughout our house. I watched as my brother and sisters collapsed like broken towers, tumbling to the floor. With each of them, went all our hopes, dreams, security, and beliefs. I felt as if I was detached from the world around me and trapped in a shriveling bubble. Everything around me looked magnified and unreal. This moment could not be happening. Maybe I am in another dream? I looked at the two younger sisters still asleep, not even flinching from all the wailing and screaming. I thought to myself again, "This must be a dream!" I then looked across the room at my Daddy, and he was slowly walking towards me. He stretched out his arms as he reached me and whispered, "I'm sorry. It's okay. You can cry." His words burst my bubble and reality hit me like a rock, as I collapsed into my Daddy's arms and cried like a baby. The unexpected, expectancy had happened, and everything played out just like Momma and I had dreamed.

The night Momma died we could not find Belinda. She had just moved to a new apartment complex, but none of us had the exact address. I remember my brother Wayne and my brother-in-law Melvin calling around and driving around the city to find the new apartments. They finally found her and brought her and her daughter Mckeeba home so that Grandma could break the news to them about Momma.

And, just like the dream, all of our Kansas and Arkansas Families and friends attended the funeral. Both mine and Momma's dreams had come true. The warning had come to both of us about what would happen. But neither of us were anyways prepared for the reality of the predictions.

I did learn that God is real and that He speaks to us in many ways. Even within a dream. I struggled for many years later with what I should have done with the prophetic knowledge that

God entrusted to me. And why He had chosen me? Could I have changed the outcome if I spoke up and told the dream to my parents? Or were the dreams just what they were - a warning? I don't believe that I will ever honestly know the answer to all my question. This was not the first communication that I had received from God and it would not be the last. I just pray as I grow in my relationship with God, that I will continue to be worthy of His leadership, insight, and understanding.

Lesson Learned: Life is a Mystery. Even when you feel you have all the answers.

Job 33:14-15 - For God does speak—now one way, now another— though no one perceives it. In a dream, in a vision of the night, when deep sleep falls on people as they slumber in their beds

---

New Beginnings

Aaron, Malisse, Miriam, Carol and Theodus

My husband, Theo and I had been married for less than a year, and I was ready to move forward with my life plan to have children. Theo wasn't in such a hurry because he already had three children from a previous relationship and marriage. Two of the kids, Ted and Shawn, visited us regularly. Ted was much like his father, very personable, and very analytical. You could tell that he would grow to be a tall, handsome man just like his dad. Shawn was a little spitfire and was always jetting around the house, flashing her big, beautiful smile. Her hazel eyes always had a spark of mischief in them. She would get this little giggle right before she did or said something ornery. Ted was Shawn's watcher, and he always tried to keep her protected. The favorite picture from our wedding was that of Theodus with tears on his face and Ted looking up at him, holding the ring pillow, with a single tear coming down his. That picture was so precious. A person could not help but fall in love with Ted and Shawn.

But being a Stepmom was challenging. There was a wiggly line that could not be crossed. I couldn't present myself as a Mom, nor as a buddy. I had to find that middle ground where I would respect them as someone else's child while still bonding with them as part of my new family. Having younger sisters around their age helped tremendously. I stumbled around in the dark here and there, but overall, I believe that it made me a better Mom.

Over a year had passed since we had said "I Do," and there still was no promise of a baby. We couldn't figure out what was going on. My doctor suggested that we might try fertility treatments. He said that these treatments were somewhat expensive and uncomfortable, but it was an option. I spoke to Theodus about our options and after much prayer, we decided that I would call the clinic on the following Monday to set an appointment to get more information.

Sundays were set as our family day. The day always began with Sunday School, Church and then a planned special day in the afternoon. That Sunday morning I was running a little late to class, so I quietly entered the back pew of the classroom as the teacher was lecturing. As I was taking my seat, a lady in front of me turned around, then loudly declared, "People run around going to fertility clinics trying to figure out why they can't get pregnant, but all they have to do is trust God!" I just stood there in shock that this woman was talking so loudly and telling my business! And how did she know I was seeing a specialist tomorrow? Then just as suddenly as the declaration began, it stopped.

I looked around, embarrassed, just knowing that everyone

in the class was now looking at me. But the crazy thing was, the class continued as if I had never entered and that an interruption had not just happened! Then the same lady who had just yelled at me turned around and said, "Oh, Hi Sister Lockhart." I was floored! What in the world was going on?? I sat in my seat, dumbfounded, not hearing a word that the teacher was saying. I was just trying to make sense of what had just happened. I finally concluded that God had just given me a spiritual message. The next morning, I called and canceled my appointment at the clinic and stepped out on faith, entrusting my future to God.

A few months had passed when we finally got the exciting news that we were three months pregnant. My husband and I celebrated the news with our families, then started exploring baby names and trying to guess if it would be a boy or a girl. We were so happy, but little did I know that this would be a very bumpy nine months.

My pregnancy journey began with a terrible bought of morning sickness. My doctor prescribed special pills to help ease my stirring tummy, but the pills made me even sicker. I was nauseated from the very start of the pregnancy to the date of delivery. Just about every smell and movement turned my stomach and sent me racing for the bathroom. I remember admiring my sister Cheryl when she was pregnant. Her hair and clothes were meticulous, and her skin had a beautiful glow. She was the perfect model of pregnancy.

Unlike Cheryl, I had morning sickness so bad that I could not stand the smell of my own clothes! My face was dry and blotchy. My hair became utterly unmanageable. And to top it off, my mouth produced a continuous stream of thick saliva, which required me to carry a spit cup like an old Hillbilly. I was what you would call a Hot Mess!! I don't know how my husband slept next to me at night. I wouldn't even want to turn over at night and see me! But he smiled at me and patted my head and kept saying, "It's going to be alright." I just could not believe that I intentionally prayed for this torture.

My mother kept me supplied with the only three food sources that I could tolerate: farm-fresh tomatoes, corn on the cob, and fresh lemons. And my Mother-in-Law ensured that I had a never-ending supply of her amazingly delicious freshly canned hot pickles. I was in heaven as long as I had these coveted items in my pantry.

About seven months into my pregnancy, December 5th, 1979, I lost my mother to undiagnosed heart disease. I went through a time of numbness and loneliness even though I had family all around me. Momma was one of my best friends. I didn't know how I was to bring a child into a world that now felt so temporary. It broke my heart that my mother would not be here to see my firstborn, and I could not imagine moving forward without her. I felt as if a curtain had been yanked shut on life. I truly believed that the sun would never shine again and that the world would settle into a perpetual state of mourning. But, to my surprise, each day the Sun somehow continued to rise and set, and the moon and stars still lit the night. Life yet happened, day in and day out, even without my mother and without my permission. It took many months to come to terms with my new life without Momma. With prayer and God's grace, my daily steps would continue to get more comfortable.

February had arrived which was the month of my due date of February 12th. I remember my friend Jolene predicted that the baby would be born on Valentine's Day, and for a moment I thought that her prediction would come true. But the baby fooled us both and was born on February 16th instead.

Months prior, my Mom and I had discussed what the delivery would be like. I believed that it would be a breeze and told her that I planned to bring a collection of my favorite magazines to help pass the time. Momma had laughed and assured me that the last thing I would be doing is reading a magazine. I was set in my belief that I could control my labor strictly through learned breathing rhythms and by keeping a positive attitude. I snubbed the stories of women who screamed and cried through labor pains. I felt it was ridiculous that a person could not go through delivery without all those antics. Momma just shook her head and said, "You will see." I thought I knew it all, but I was so very naive and uneducated about bringing forth life. I remember the day my fantasies exploded, and the lights came on.

My husband and I had gone to our Lamaze Class to learn the breathing techniques for having a natural delivery. Since I had a high pain tolerance, I was convinced that I would not need to have any pain medication during labor. I wanted my child's delivery to be completely natural. Near the end of the class, the instructor showed a film of actual childbirth. Everything was going fine until it got to the part of the actual delivery. I remember sitting straight up in my chair, throwing my hand over my mouth, then loudly cried, "OH MY GOD! THAT'S HOW THE BABY IS COMING OUT!" I felt my head swim, and at first, I thought I was going to pass out. I looked at my husband, then to the instructor, and declared, "I AM NOT DOING THIS!" I felt betrayed. Why hadn't anyone told me what was going to happen? The whole class broke into laughter. I had presented myself as a Ms. Know-it-all, now I was showing my stupidity to everyone.

The instructor calmly asked, "How did you think the baby would get here, Carol?" My ignorance was on a roll now, and I could not stop it. I responded, "I don't know! I thought something would open up, and the baby would drop out." By now, the others in the class were hysterical and in tears from laughing so hard. All I knew was that on T.V., they rolled the Mom-to-be into a room, then a few minutes later, they would present a baby.

Momma was the first one I called with my newfound knowledge. When she answered, I shrieked, "Do you know how this baby is coming out of me!" Momma just laughed uncontrollably and responded, "So, which magazines did you want to take to delivery?" I was in total shock. I remember thinking about the process of delivery all night. I felt I had to educate everyone about what I had learned. So, as soon as I arrived at work, I shared my new-found knowledge with all the ladies in my office. Of course, this started another round of laughter. How did everyone know how babies were born except me? At that time, I had less than a month before my due date to digest and come to terms with my fate.

Delivery day came, and Momma had been right. I did not

have time to read magazines. The pain was horrifying. At one point, I heard myself begging the doctor to "Just cut her out!" I felt like my body was turning inside out. My husband swore that he heard me speak a different language and that my head spun around on my body while oozing green bile out of my mouth. I'm sure he exaggerated. But I don't know because it was intense. All I know was that the experience was nothing like I had ever imagined.

My labor pains were coming every 3-5 minutes for 15 hours. At around the seven-hour mark, an arrogant doctor came in and without notice pushed down extremely hard on my stomach, which was his way of forcing the baby further down the birth canal. My reflex with his actions was to kick. And he caught the kick hard. A shouting match ensued, followed by him storming out not to return. The nurses were stunned and wondered why he would do something so cruel.

Finally, eight hours later, it was time to push. The nurses wheeled me down the hall to the delivery room, which would be the final stage of this ordeal. Theo was positioned behind me. His job was to keep me on track with my Lamaze breathing and to lift me forward when it was time to push. But each time I was ready to push, Theodus would get so excited he would push me forward before I could get a breath. It felt like the top of my head was going to pop off and spin on the floor. We finally got synchronized with our breathing and pushing, and before long, our beautiful baby girl was born. To the astonishment of the doctors, she was born face up, with her eyes wide open.

Our baby was exquisite. She had gorgeous reddish-brown skin with beautiful long coal-black hair that hung almost to the middle of her back. She was perfect and well worth the long nine months of morning sickness, stiff back, Charlie horse plagued legs, out of control hair and smelly clothes. She was worth every pain, every stretch mark, and every pound gained. She was priceless, and I loved her at first sight. I could not believe that God had entrusted us with such an amazing little person. The nurses fell in love with her also, and she became their living baby doll. Every time they brought her into my room, she would have a different little hairstyle. When it came time for us to leave for home, they all lined up to give her a final kiss and hug goodbye.

Our family had now been extended to include our first child. We had decided months earlier that her name would be Ashley Nicole, but about a month before her birth, we had been inspired to change it to Miriam Renee'.

In the months to come I would learn a lot about babies and how to change diapers, clean and boil bottles and mix and heat up formula. By the time we had our second daughter (Malisse) three years later, I was a pro. Malisse was different in appearance and personalization. Malisse had barely brown skin, brownish-blonde wavy hair, and blue eyes. Miriam was a very peaceful baby, and Malisse demanded her way in all things. She earned the title of 'Little Grumpy Bear," after the Care Bear toys.

A year after Malisse was born came our son Aaron. He was born with a thick layer of scaly skin all over his body. I never have seen anything like it. I attributed it to all the seafood I craved and ate while carrying him. Aaron had light brown eyes and curly brown hair and his skin was as white as eggshells. Which is funny because he hated eggs. Theodus was a little startled and even gave me a side-eye on that one. But I just laughed and said, "He's Yours!"

God blessed us with three beautiful, intelligent, fun, spirited children. Theodus's oldest daughter Glenda had come into our lives a little before Malisse was born. So, the Lockhart crew multiplied from four to six to eight. Even though we did not all live in the same home, we were still family. I always joked that my husband had copy-cat kids because though they were 12 years apart, each group matched the other. Ted and Aaron look alike, talk alike, walk alike. Shawn and Malisse both have sandy colored hair, crazy beautiful hazel eyes, and feisty personalities. Glenda and Miriam look alike with the same gorgeous skin color, infectious smile and long, thick, dark wavy hair. When they are all together, it is almost impossible to tell that they have different mothers.

Ted, Shawn, and Glenda ended up moving to Denver, CO, with their mothers. And our part of the family ended up in Wichita, KS due to relocation of Theodus's job. There are so many more stories to tell about my adventures as a wife and parent. But those will come as we are, "Still Learning in 316."

To Be Continued...

Colossians 3:14
"And above all these put on love, which binds
everything together in perfect harmony."

Printed in the United States
By Bookmasters